CW00540837

"I have read the book twice. I am starting it again shortly as **every time I read it I get something new from it**. Also, and here is the real secret, when you start to act on what the book says, its content becomes even more relevant.

"Many would say, 'I already know that'. But if you did know, why haven't you done something about it? With the help in this book you no longer have any excuses!"

Steve Wilson
Thieme & Co
Sheffield

"Once again Richard and Steve show an ability to get to the heart of the issues which affect all accountancy practices. Their **easy and simple style** will appeal to any reader, and will have them rushing to implement the many ideas - just do it!"

Ian Mitchell
Mitchell Meredith Ltd
Powys

"If you just do one thing, make sure you read this book. **This system has worked wonders for us**. Let's hope my competitors don't read it. I have been using the full system for 6 months and the results have been beyond amazing."

Andy Page
PH Accountancy Ltd
Whitstable

"This book sets out some home truths that any Accountancy Practice will ignore at its own peril. It is not only fascinating but it provides a framework to succeed, and my Practice is now following it."

Andrew Gerrard
Harding Lewis Chartered Accountants
Douglas, Isle of Man

"These are exciting times for us in the development of our business and the insights gained from Steve and Richard's book are **invaluable to us in ensuring that we optimise our plan and stick to it in terms of its development**. We very much endorse the messages contained in the book."

John Campbell
Managing Director - DSC Chartered Accountants
Harrogate

"Torr Waterfield have been AFG members for over a year and the business growth services have really **helped our practice** and our clients over the last 12 months.

"AFG has helped our practice and our clients in obtaining **more profitable business and customers** together with the systemisation of a sales and marketing strategy.

"Steve Hackney and Richard Brewin have first-hand experience in growing successful accountancy practices and come highly recommended – and so does this book."

Tom Simpson FCA
Director - Torr Waterfield Accountants
Leicester

"How To Quickly Grow Your Accountancy Practice really does **demystify the 'dark art' of getting new clients** and I'm no longer overwhelmed by the prospect of growing my practice. I am totally convinced that a practice following the programme set out by Steve and Richard in this book **cannot fail to grow**."

John Elstub
Crimson Harvest
St Ives

"Before I read 'How To Quickly Grow Your Accountancy Practice' by Steve Hackney and Richard Brewin I thought that marketing was an art which was why I was not very good at it. As an accountant, being a numerate person, I had none of the artistic and literary skills needed to be good at marketing. The main lesson that I have learned from Steve and Richard is that **marketing is less of an art and more of a science**.

"If you follow well-designed and tested procedures in your marketing you can deliver a predictable outcome and indeed pick up much more work of the type you want. Not only do Steve and Richard get this message over in an expert manner, they **actually teach you** how to apply the **five Ms of marketing** and those crucial **nine Marketing Assets** that have to be present in every single media piece for it to be successful.

"I have long been aware of the need for effective marketing in the accountancy profession. Steve Hackney and Richard Brewin explain lucidly exactly how to do it."

John Harrison
John Harrison and Company Chartered Accountants
Worksop

"A **simple and easy-to-use system**, which takes you through both the 'why' and the 'how' of growing your accountancy practice. I would urge **anyone who is serious about growing their accountancy practice** to make time in your busy schedule to read this book because if you put in place even a handful of these ideas you will start to see **immediate improvements** in the success of your marketing function."

Andy Irvine
Shorts Chartered Accountants
Chesterfield

"At last! As accountants we train for years to pass exams, to learn to practise 'ethically' and are required to keep our knowledge and specialisms up-to-date.

"**The missing piece of the jigsaw is how to market our services**. After qualifying we are 'cut loose' and expected to not only grow our own business with real knowledge of how to do it, but today we are expected to advise our clients how to do it. Scary thoughts!

"Steve and Richard's book provides an excellent, **easy-to-understand** but more importantly **easy-to-implement, step-by-step guide as to 'how' to grow our accountancy practices**.

"Many accountants are not natural 'marketeers' and this book will prove to be an invaluable addition to our library.

"Yes, it takes us out of our comfort zone but explains in easy, well set out chapters the **essential steps** we all need to take to grow a successful, profitable firm."

Steve Taylor
Kis Accounting Limited
Taunton

How To Quickly Grow Your Accountancy Practice

FIRST EDITION

By acquiring and keeping the clients you REALLY want

Steve Hackney &
Richard Brewin

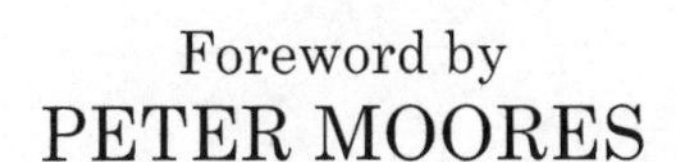

Foreword by
PETER MOORES

AFG
PUBLISHING

How To Quickly Grow Your Accountancy Practice

By Acquiring And Keeping The Clients You Really Want

Steve Hackney & Richard Brewin

ISBN 978-0-9567907-0-5

Published by:

AFG Publishing
Academy For Growth Ltd
Suites 1-10, Springfield House
Water Lane
Wilmslow
United Kingdom
SK9 5BG

UK: 0844 44 80 640
International: +44 1625 88 65 88
Web: www.AcademyForGrowth.co.uk

FOREWORD

Success is about having a "Point of Difference"

"If you always do what you always did, then you will always get what you always got."

By Peter Moores
(Former England Cricket Coach and now Head Coach at Lancashire CCC)

You may be wondering why a cricket coach is writing the foreword to a book on accounting practice...

Well it isn't that I've suddenly decided to change professions, though after spending some time with Steve and Richard their principles apply equally to sport as well as business.

The World is changing at a rate that is staggering and the solutions of yesterday are often not good enough to face the challenges of tomorrow.

In this book, Steve and Richard have put in place a step-by-step guide to help you through the process of change and come up with innovative ideas that are both simple and practical.

Like all good things their solutions make real sense and for those who are brave enough to take on the challenge of change, the rewards are often significant.

So how does this book connect to sport and what I do for a living?

In sport and most high-end activities, we are all looking for that "point of difference". Something that sets you apart from the rest, whilst giving you the edge required for success. In sport we have players and coaches looking for all sorts of weird and wonderful ways to find the winning formula, though in truth the gimmicks are always found out.

The pathway to success in sport is to have talented players with the necessary "basics", which they can deliver at pace and adapt to any given situation.

Hence the connection with Steve's background in elite rugby, allied to his experience in the field of marketing. This is combined with the wealth of knowledge that Richard has gained over his years as an accountant and his experience using these principles and methods, not once but twice.

This combination has produced a set of basics for building your accountancy business, which will take you through the different stages of growth.

Their unique approach takes you into the boardroom, allowing you to compare conventional practice or perceived wisdom against the possibilities of taking the road less-travelled. The journey is full of common sense that has evolved through their hours of research and the successful practices they have retained along the way.

I spend a lot of my time challenging the players, the support staff and myself to evaluate our current situation to ensure we are moving with the times, knowing that if you stand still you can get overtaken.

We are always looking to improve whilst maintaining the solid foundations needed for sustained growth.

This book provides a way forward for those who are willing to embrace a new approach and I am confident that it will give you the "point of difference" that we are all hoping to find.

PREFACE

A friend of ours was looking stressed. Yet again his accountant had let him down, failing to tell him about a problem with his records. He could have sorted it out himself if he'd known, but his accountant had taken it upon himself and sent him a big bill instead. "Why don't you get yourself a new accountant?" we said. "You have problems every year with these guys." "What's the point?" he sighed. "They're all the same, aren't they?"

It's a common view. Like banks, all accountants are the same in the eyes of many. On one level you can see why the general business community would think this. Accountancy firms all provide the same basic compliance services of accounts and tax; the same support services of payroll, bookkeeping, etc. Everyone talks about being proactive, about being partner-led. Offers of a free introductory meeting are commonplace. Unfortunately so are the criticisms of expense, lack of value, lack of service and lack of care.

Yet it's not true. As you read this you will already be saying, "Ah yes, but that's not us. We're different." We meet hundreds of accountants every year and most believe that their firm offers something different.

So, why the anomaly? Why does the general view differ from the professional's perspective? This book sets out to show why accountancy firms fail to create the right impression, thus impacting on their ability to gain and retain the right sort of clients. More importantly, we will show you exactly what you can do about it. We will show you how to market and grow your accountancy practice in a simple, cost-effective and time-efficient manner that will once and for all establish the right perception of your firm across your market place.

Each chapter will introduce simple and effective methods and tools for growth that will cost very little or, more commonly, nothing at all and, perhaps more importantly, use the minimum amount of your time.

The methods we use in this book will apply to every accountancy practice, regardless of the number of partners or the types of clients. Whether you are a sole practitioner or a partner in a global practice, this is relevant to you. However, to demonstrate where the profession is now, and the impact of our methods, we will use two imaginary practices throughout this book. Let us introduce you:

Grey & Black Accountants and AFG Accountants LLP are, today, identical practices. Both are two-partner firms operating from High Street offices in the same town. Both have been going for ten years, have grown to 220 clients in that time and have five staff. Both have found growth difficult in the last couple of years and, whilst neither have any retention problems yet (although they do lose clients every year), the frustrations are growing. The hopes of the early years are starting to fade. What new business they do get comes mainly from referrals and general marketing is largely avoided as it's seen as ineffective.

Both firms have a partners' meeting today with the objective being...

"Where do we go from here?"

Each chapter of the book addresses each agenda point. The first being – 'Why Has Our Growth Slowed?'. This is where our journey together begins...

AGENDA

Agenda Item 1

1. Introduction

Just over 8 months ago on a cold frosty morning, the partners of two virtually identical accountancy firms came to the uncomfortable conclusion that their firms were no longer growing. Or at least not growing at the rate they wanted. Or growing with the wrong type of clients.

You've already been introduced to these firms: Black & Grey Accountants and AFG Accountants LLP.

They're not alone.

According to Key Note there were 33,270 accountancy firms by the end of 2009. Two-thirds (62.5%) of these firms generated a turnover of less than £100,000 in 2009, and 32.1% of those recorded a turnover of less than £50,000. Only 16.2% declared a turnover of £250,000 or more in 2009, while just 3.8% had a turnover of £1m or more.

In its 2010 report, Key Note points out that during 2009 the number of firms with a turnover of less than £50,000 increased by 3%. More interestingly, fee income dropped 3% to £21.4billion in 2009 with little hope of a significant change of fortunes predicted in 2010.

This drop of 3% is the first time in 5 years the profession has seen a decline in fee income and with 2011 showing only a very small growth in the overall economy and 2012 not looking much better, accountants face a challenging time ahead to grow their firms.

A wise man once said, "If you've stopped growing, you're actually shrinking." Nothing is more fundamentally true when it comes to an accountancy practice. If you're not acquiring new

clients then you are almost certainly going backwards. Even if you are great at servicing clients you will always lose a small number through mergers, acquisitions, retirement, bankruptcy (more so at the moment), death and relocation.

So alarmingly, if your firm has slowed it won't be long before it starts going backwards, just like our two case study firms.

However, the good news is, with the right advice and good old-fashioned hard work you can buck this trend and create a fast-growing and dominant firm. A firm that grows month on month. A firm that not only works with the right type of clients – but works with the clients you really want.

That's why we wrote this book.

Surprisingly, our research showed very little in the way of support for accountants looking to grow their firms. Certainly nothing of any note that had been written in the last ten years or so. Maybe this is a result of the industry's general success over the last twenty years. Maybe it wasn't needed. Maybe complacency had set in?

Without question, the baby boom of the 60s and early 70s has led to a very large number of firms being created. Supply has finally outstripped demand. More alarmingly, the customer has become more discerning. So competition is rife and acquiring the client is harder than ever.

But just when you thought it couldn't get any worse...

To top all of that, most business owners think that accountants are now like the banks – they're all the same. And guess what? This means if they think one firm is the same as the next – they then choose on price. So through the industry's own apathy it has created a price-sensitive market. It's a grim picture.

Of course it's only grim if you do nothing about it. Remember, if you keep doing what you've always done, you'll get what you always got.

You bought this book because you see it as the first step of doing something about it. We of course don't know your exact personal situation, but we do know you want improvement in your firm. And we do know for whatever reason you're not happy with things as they stand at the moment. Realising this, as our two firms have done, is part of the battle.

Next it's all about what you do about it. You need to get busy and start implementing a range of strategies that will help you...

- Stand out from the crowd
- Attract clients easily
- Remove price and fee from the mind of the client
- Provide added value that no other firm can compete with
- Acquire the right type of clients at the right fees
- Achieve everything your skills, effort and experience deserve

That's why this book is so important. It's to give you proven solutions to each and every one of these things. But be warned. Although growing your firm is down to some basic fundamentals, many of the things we talk to you about will fly in the face of what you believe to be true. You have to trust us. This stuff works. It doesn't matter if you're a sole trader or in a firm with three or twenty-three partners. But to get results you have to change what you're doing. You have to be different. You cannot hope to achieve all you want with an attitude of 'this will never work for my firm'. You have to open your mind to the opportunities that present themselves to you in this book. And if you do, then you're going to enjoy the results of your efforts. We promise you that.

So let's get started. We've given you full access to each partner meeting. Black & Grey Accountants are going it alone. AFG Accountants LLP have invited us both to help them.

Enjoy the journey...

AGENDA ITEM 2

2. WHY HAS OUR GROWTH SLOWED?

INTRODUCTION

To understand why growth slows or stagnates in any accountancy firm, we first need to look at how a typical firm evolves and why the frustration starts to mount as this growth slows. We call this the 'Growth Roller-Coaster'.

Take a look at the illustration below.

THE GROWTH ROLLER COASTER

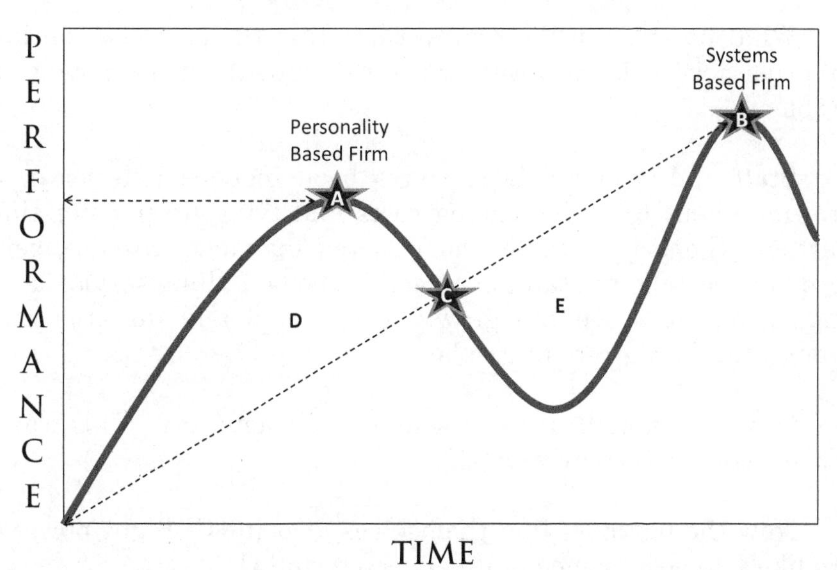

The starting point is the beginning of an accountancy practice, usually created by a sole practitioner or a small partnership. Typically, the partners are very hands-on at this stage with few, if any, staff and modest resources. In the early months and years the firm grows very well.

Clients receive a high degree of partner attention with high levels of expertise and client-care as a result. Costs in the modest operation are relatively low and the firm can respond quickly to client and market needs.

Word is spread by clients and referrers about the great, cost-effective service and new business is easily gained. The practice quickly expands to a peak at point **A**, driven by the personalities and skills of its owning partners.

In an ideal world, two conditions will now be met. Firstly, the partners will recognise that they have reached the pinnacle for a personality-driven business and secondly, the business and financial performance will be at a level that completely satisfies them. In reality, neither is the case.

What happens in the real world is that the partners continue to drive forward. However, with the growth there now come problems...

Staff and resource levels have been increased to serve the growing client base, increasing costs and tying up partner time. Partners themselves come under increasing time pressure, being torn between client, staff and practice needs. Falling service levels and rising costs see the growth constricted and dissatisfaction around the firm grows in its place.

Have you ever heard yourself or a colleague say, "This was so much easier in the early days!"

Now the partners find themselves at point **C**. Right now, you are likely to be at some point between **A** and **C**.

Reality has dawned and the firm is at a crossroads. Do you remain a personality-driven practice and attempt to claw your way back to point **A** by downsizing, culling clients and try and raise point A to a higher pinnacle? Or, do you undertake the investment (mostly in time and effort) required to move forward to become a systems-based firm at point C. **Since you're reading this book it's highly likely this is what you want to achieve**.

Interestingly both types of firm can be successful with the right planning and management. However, too many firms find themselves falling into the trough in between simply because they've not considered early enough what their fundamental strategies and goals will be. So much emphasis is placed upon the process functions, delivering compliance, support and advisory services to clients that the essential marketing (taken care of in this book) and management of the business itself is overlooked (see diagrams on next page). Growth, consequently, is flawed.

Let's look then at the high-level view of your firm (any accountancy firm). As we mentioned above, it has three key components...

1. **Process**
   The mechanics by which an accountancy practice 'produces' its saleable services – compliance, support and advisory.

2. **Marketing**
   The generation of new clients, the retention of existing clients and the maximisation of client value (this book focuses on this second component).

3. **Management**
   The running of the business – its performance management, strategies and goals.

Let's take a closer look at what this looks like...

MANAGEMENT FUNCTION	PROCESS FUNCTION	MARKETING FUNCTION
Administration	Compliance Services	Sales
Processes	Support Services	Marketing
Systems	Advisory Services	Retention
Staff Development	Specialist Services	
↓	↓	↓
PROFIT & WEALTH	FEES	CLIENTS

When a firm is growing steadily and reaching the partners' objectives, the 3 functions work together to create a harmonious cycle...

In reality, the majority of Partners are taught process skills from school days, through professional studies and onwards. We are taught how to read and write. How to do sums and answer questions. You develop expertise in how to do 'things'.

In other words, your expertise and skills invariably lie in the **PROCESS** function. Consequently, with the skills and knowledge loaded towards the Process function, firms can only grow whilst there is capacity within the Process function to do so.

But **without** the same relative development in the management and in particular marketing functions either side, **growth becomes limited...**

The cycle now starts to look very different...

So the solution is simple...

You need to start putting more effort into the marketing and management functions of the firm to realign the balance.

This doesn't mean you neglect the process function. It just means you work smarter and allocate your time and effort better to include these two crucial areas of your practice.

So, there is little doubt as to why most firms do not achieve the growth objectives the partners have set and why now is the time to make the transition from a process-led firm to a management- and, in particular, a marketing-led firm.

Our goal is for you to have a systems-based firm that is set up to achieve your objectives. The rest of this book shows you how to achieve growth through a series of proven sales and marketing strategies that you can automate.

BLACK & GREY ACCOUNTANTS

Of course Black & Grey know their growth has slowed, but they put it down to the economy. There's no need to panic. It's tough for everyone. Things will turn around and they've not lost that many clients... yet. Yes, as we saw with the Key Note figures, the economy has played a part, but only a small part. The big reason for its slowdown is how the firm is marketed.

Black & Grey, in fairness, know they're not doing enough marketing. So on the basis of 'we need to do more marketing' they move on to agenda item 3.

AFG ACCOUNTANTS LLP

"So you see, you've reached point C on the 'Growth Roller-Coaster', that's why your firm has slowed in its growth. Now you understand why this has happened you're in a much better position to do something about it.

"What we want to make clear is you have absolutely no control over outside forces such as the economy, the competition, and low-price competition. You can only control what you do and by taking control you can minimise and virtually eliminate the effect of these non-controllable market forces.

"So now you have a good grasp of why the firm has slowed in its growth, let's look at how you can grow the firm."

KEY SUMMARY & ACTION POINTS

1. Re-read this section to fully understand why your firm has stopped growing.

2. Take responsibility for the position your firm is in. You cannot and must not blame anything outside your control. You (and any other partners) are and must be the only person who can drive your firm forward.

3. Understand that as long as you have the right attitude (this WILL work for me rather than this will never work in my business) then no matter where your firm is on the Growth Roller-Coaster you can take steps to overcome any challenge you have by implementing the advice in this book.

AGENDA ITEM 3

3. HOW DO WE GROW OUR FIRM?

INTRODUCTION

The good news is that growing any accountancy firm comes down to some sound basic fundamentals, some of which you will have been exposed to before and others you won't.

Now remember, our goal is to help you create a system-led firm on autopilot, so the growth of the firm has to be based around an easy-to-apply marketing system.

We'll show you the system first, and then we can explain it in more detail. Here's what your system should look like (see next page).

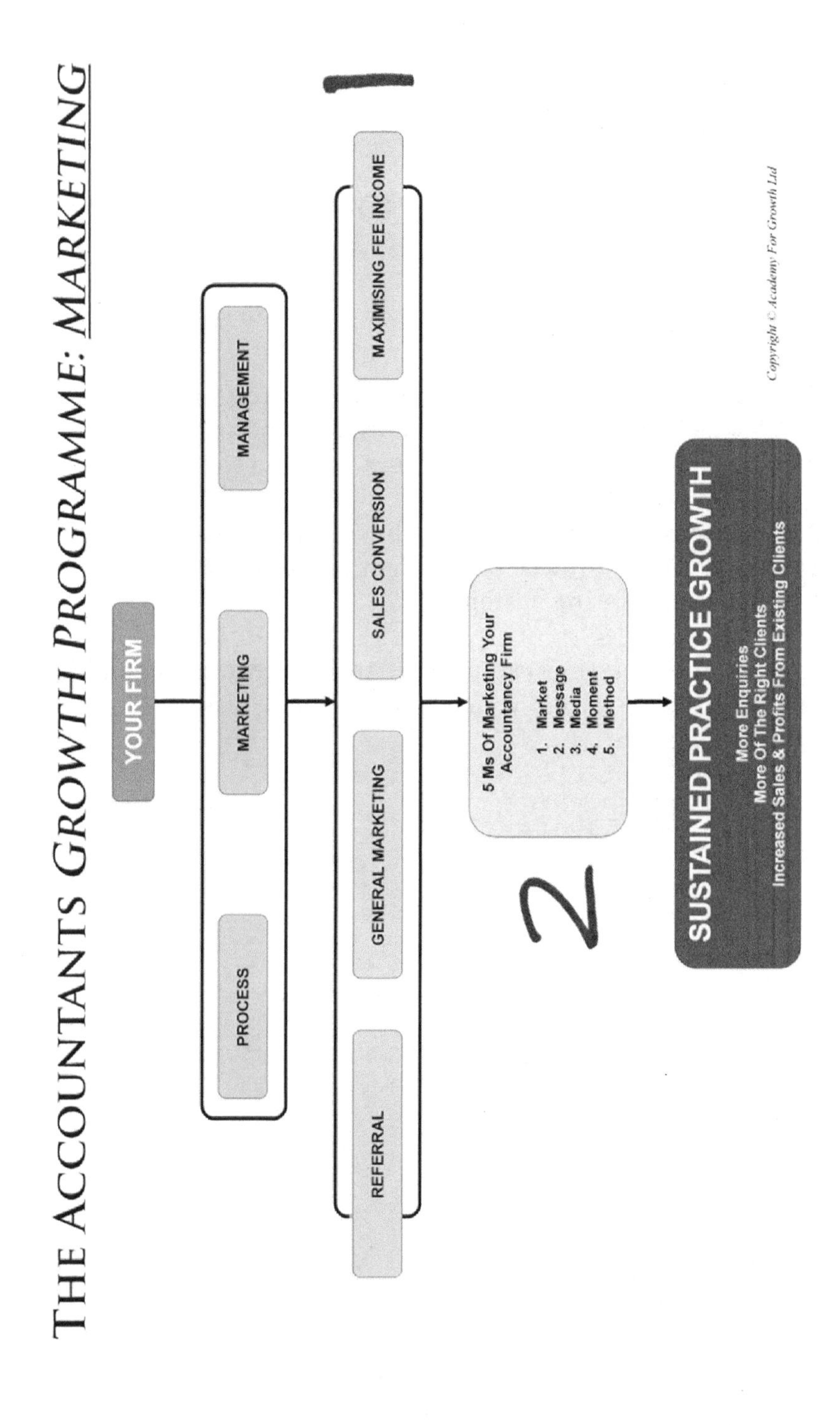
THE ACCOUNTANTS GROWTH PROGRAMME: MARKETING
YOUR FIRM
PROCESS
MARKETING
MANAGEMENT
REFERRAL
GENERAL MARKETING
SALES CONVERSION
MAXIMISING FEE INCOME
5 Ms Of Marketing Your Accountancy Firm
1. Market
2. Message
3. Media
4. Moment
5. Method
SUSTAINED PRACTICE GROWTH
More Enquiries
More Of The Right Clients
Increased Sales & Profits From Existing Clients
Copyright © Academy For Growth Ltd

As you can see there are actually just two 'levels' to a powerful marketing system and when they're combined you create a practice that keeps growing and growing. Let's take a closer look at each level...

1. **'The 4 Practice Multipliers' (4 Ways To Grow Your Firm):**

   Other than acquisition of other firms or blocks of fees, there are just 4 ways to grow your accountancy firm...

   - Referral: We all know that generating enquiries by referral is THE single best way to get clients. However, virtually every accountancy firm has what we call a 'reactive referral process' in place. This ISN'T a system. This 'ad hoc' approach will only get you so far, but when you want to achieve growth targets you cannot hope to grow your firm on this basis. The key word in all of this (which you'll hear a lot from us) is ***SYSTEM***. Systemising your referrals from clients and other third-party referral sources such as IFAs and solicitors is key to your success.

   - General Marketing: Rigorous testing has provided us with a number of proven marketing approaches which enable accountancy firms to generate many enquiries at will. The reason why most firms believe that general marketing is often ineffective is explained in (2) below.

     However, a critical piece of the success jigsaw is to use a number of marketing approaches, not just one or two (another key reason why most firms don't grow at the rate they should).

     We have a saying: "Other than zero, the worst number in business is '1'; 1 key client, 1 key supplier, 1 key employee and 1 marketing approach." You are seriously harming your firm if you only use one or two marketing approaches (another big cause of growth slowing).

- Sales Conversion: When your referral and general marketing systems are operating effectively, they will generate a healthy supply of enquiries every month. As soon as an enquiry is generated your 'sales conversion system' should kick in.

  In other words, you should have a system in place that helps the prospective client through your sales process, ensuring they become a client. (Yes we've dared to use the word 'sales' in this book. Whether you like it or not you have to sell, but by using a system you take the skill factor out of the equation, so even once poorly performing partners or managers can convert at a much higher level.)

  You need to build in a number of stages, whereby each one moves the prospective client closer to the sale. Once again this is a BIG weakness we see in most firms – there isn't usually any kind of sales conversion system in place.

  We have come across firms who were only converting 1 in 10 enquiries (from general marketing enquiries) prior to implementing a sales conversion system. Take note that we are talking about true conversion rates here. Many firms kid themselves that their conversion rates are higher than they actually are because they only count the 'easy' pickings from warm referrals and ignore all the failed general marketing efforts. Once the system was in place they improved their conversion to between 7 and 9 out of 10.

  This makes a huge difference to your new client acquisitions – and is achieved with absolutely ZERO extra cost.

- Maximising Fee Income: Much has been written and spoken about selling more services to existing clients. In reality many firms find this one of their most challenging tasks. But it needn't be so. The reality is that most firms just miss so many golden opportunities to up-sell and cross-sell their services, again because no formal system is in place for actually doing it.

You know as well as we do that little thought is ever given to putting in place a solid system that identifies the opportunities for selling more services to clients and what exactly has to be done when these opportunities arise.

> IMPORTANT NOTE:
>
> As you can imagine, just small improvements across each of the 4 Practice Multipliers will result in big increases in growth. That's the power of the practice multipliers.

2. <u>The 5 Ms Of Marketing Your Accountancy Firm:</u>

So you know that there are 4 ways to grow your firm. However, this still isn't enough. Each of these methods must be underpinned by a set of time-tested rules which ensure their success. We call these the '5 Ms of Marketing Your Accountancy Firm' (Market, Message, Media, Moment and Method)...

- <u>Market:</u> Who you are targeting (your 'Target Market').

- <u>Message:</u> Why someone should use your firm rather than anyone else (your competitors) and what you need to convey in your message to get people to respond and buy.

- <u>Media:</u> The marketing channels you will use to deliver your message to the market (i.e. website, adverts, direct mail, articles, etc.).

- <u>Moment:</u> Timing is everything!

- Method: What 'marketing piece' will you use for each media, to rise above the clutter and get noticed over EVERY other business that's marketing to your target market (notice this is other accountants AND every other type of business trying to get your potential clients to buy from them).

So there you have it. That's what it takes to grow any accountancy firm – no matter where you are in your evolution. No matter how long you've been established. No matter what your goals and objectives are. This is the system that will bring you the results you need.

BLACK & GREY ACCOUNTANTS

Like most firms, Black & Grey don't utilise all 4 of the Practice Growth Multipliers, nor do they understand or appreciate why the 5 Ms Of Marketing An Accountancy Practice play such an important part in acquiring and retaining the right clients.

This ignorance and lack of knowledge means they will never reach their potential. Worse still, it could mean that everything they try to implement from this day forward simply won't work (or work as well as it should)!

They complete this part of the meeting by agreeing that they need to do more 'marketing' (which means they are going to focus on how to generate more enquiries).

However, and thankfully, they recognise the need to at least try and target the right people for their firm.

AFG ACCOUNTANTS LLP

"We said none of this was rocket science. Now you've seen the Accountants Growth System and you understand the basics of each element, hopefully you can see that its success lies in its simplicity.

"But we guarantee as long as you apply each element to your firm, you will see the growth that you seek.

"However, the scale of your success depends on how well you execute each of the elements in the system. So let's take a look at the first and most important part of growing your practice – the target market."

KEY SUMMARY & ACTION POINTS

1. **1.** Re-read this section to fully understand the two key components of your practice growth system.
2. **2.** Understand that for your practice to grow and dominate your competition, you need a marketing system that runs on autopilot.
3. **3.** Appreciate that improving every component by just a small fraction will have a big overall impact on your firm as a whole.

AGENDA ITEM 4

4. HOW DO WE ACQUIRE THE RIGHT CLIENTS FOR US?

INTRODUCTION

To get the best possible results from each of the Practice Multipliers and all the marketing pieces you use you must first, and most importantly, clearly identify the type(s) of businesses you are looking to target. These are known as 'target markets'.

> The ideal Target Market is a clearly identified group(s) of people / organisations who/which...
>
> **1.** Need – and more accurately 'want' – your services
>
> **2.** Can afford to pay for your services
>
> **3.** Can be easily reached by your marketing efforts
>
> **4.** Have similarities (demographic/psychographic) that enable you to 'group' them together

One of the biggest mistakes you can make is to try and be 'all things to all men'. Yes, there is success to be found using this approach, but by focusing on one or more carefully chosen 'target markets' or 'niches' you'll be far more successful, and this success will be achieved much quicker than with any other approach.

So why do so many accountancy firms try to be all things to all men? In most cases it's because they're frightened to 'limit' the number of businesses they specifically target. They think if they reduce the number of prospects, they'll risk their whole livelihood!

Nothing could be further from the truth. Let us explain...

We're often asked – "If I limit my market, won't I be reducing the chances of doing business with more people?"

Yes you will. But to succeed in today's competitive market place you need to concentrate your marketing on a small number of well-chosen target markets, into which you pour all of your resources.

Of course, if you focus on a smaller group(s) you may miss the business from outside the target group. But what actually happens is you increase the amount of business you receive from the target group.

This is because you are specifically meeting the niche market's needs and requirements. You are saying to them that you are THE accountant who knows about their situation – their problems – and their concerns. No other accountant specifically meets their needs in this way and therefore the firm is seen as the logical company to turn to.

So you must define who your target market is BEFORE you do anything else.

TRADITIONAL MASS MARKETING VERSUS TARGET OR NICHE MARKETING...

The diagram on the next page clearly shows the differences between conventional marketing (mass marketing) and 'world-class' marketing that we adhere to (target marketing)...

4. How Do We Acquire The Right Clients For Us?

The Mass Marketing Approach

Businesses Who Are Unlikely To Buy

The white space represents businesses that are unlikely to buy, but they all receive the same marketing message from the business which results in needless and excessive expense.

The Market Universe

The prospects who could buy your accountancy services – 'Mass Market'.

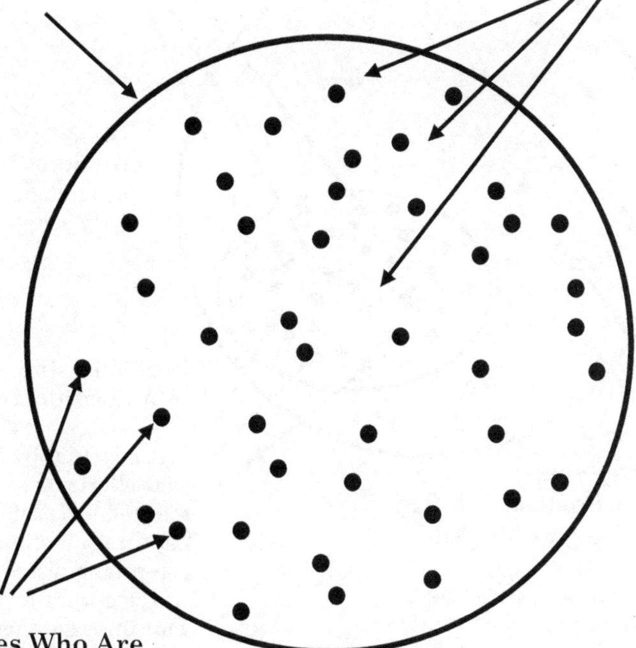

Businesses Who Are In A Position To Buy

Note how disparate these are. The white space in between represents everyone else in the mass market. You have to spend much more money to get 'lucky' and hit the right people/businesses.

The Result

High cost to reach buyers. Response and acquisitions are low because you're targeting everyone with a 'mass market' message – i.e. it doesn't directly appeal to the buyers. Greater effort (on your part!) required to qualify out bad prospects – if you're targeting everyone, you'll also get a large number of poor prospects and YOU DON'T WANT THAT!

THE TARGET OR NICHE MARKET APPROACH

The Market Universe

The businesses who <u>could</u> buy your accountancy services – 'Mass Market'.

Businesses Who Are Unlikely To Buy

The white space represents businesses who are still unlikely to buy, but they all receive the tailored marketing message from you once the enquiry has been generated by your marketing efforts. Notice there are fewer now!

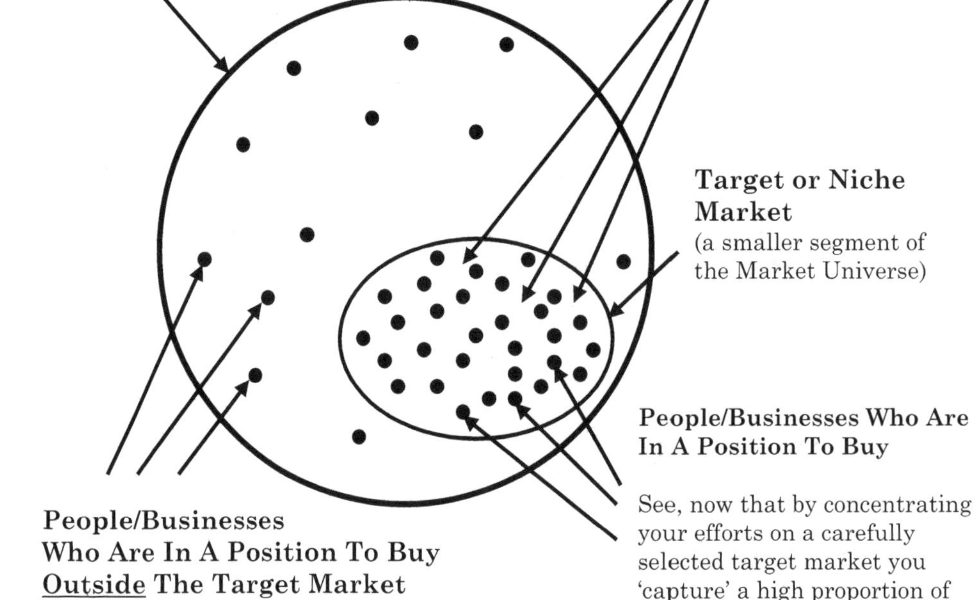

Target or Niche Market

(a smaller segment of the Market Universe)

People/Businesses Who Are In A Position To Buy

See, now that by concentrating your efforts on a carefully selected target market you 'capture' a high proportion of potential buyers. Plus, once you've generated the enquiry your message then also needs to be completely focused on this group so client acquisitions are increased significantly.

People/Businesses Who Are In A Position To Buy <u>Outside</u> The Target Market

Even this approach isn't perfect – but it's close! You can't hope to 'catch' everyone. There will still be other people/businesses outside the chosen niche(s) that you 'miss'. But notice how few there are.

The Result

This gives you the ability to concentrate your efforts on a more targeted group. Target marketing increases the likelihood of a sale. And enables YOU to take a big slice of this target market.

Multiple Target Or Niche Markets

You don't have to restrict yourself to just one target market. You may find it necessary to focus on two or more target markets depending on the service you provide. For example, you may have three target markets...

- Primary - Start-up businesses
- Secondary - £1 to £2m businesses
- Tertiary - £2m - £5m businesses

...or even more 'vertical' (defined)...

- Primary - Dentists
- Secondary - Media companies
- Tertiary - Legal

You would need to 'speak' and 'communicate' very differently to each target market once the enquiry has been generated because they are so different. You cannot speak the same way to a start-up business as you would a £5m business – so why do people do it?

Here's a diagram showing how this looks...

MULTIPLE TARGET MARKETS

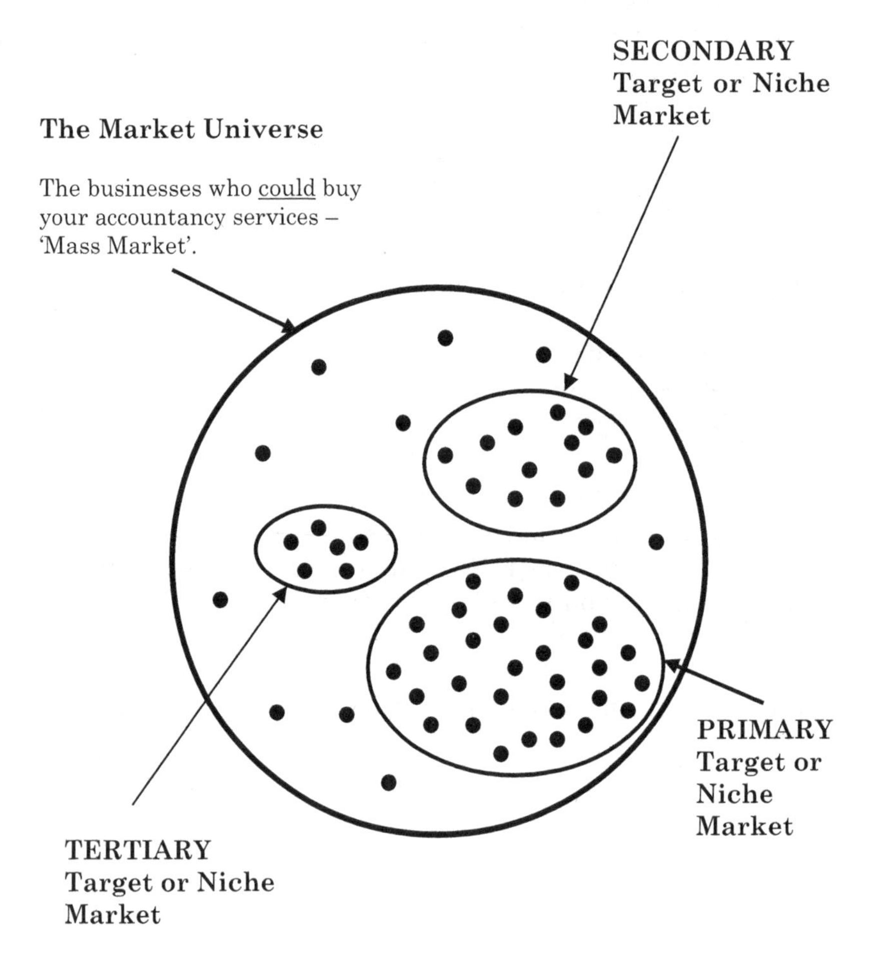

The Result

This gives you the ability to concentrate your efforts on more targeted groups. Target marketing increases the likelihood of a sale. And enables YOU to take a big slice of this target market.

4. How Do We Acquire The Right Clients For Us?

The Power Of Target Marketing

Here's a simple but very powerful example of why defining your target market or niche is so important...

Let's say a start-up business needs an accountant. Their first choice is to look in the Yellow Pages under the 'Accountancy' category. Although there are a number of ads, the first one reads...

> 'ABC Chartered Accountants. Tax preparation, auditing, bookkeeping, payroll services, help for start-ups, management accounts, and so on.'

The second ad reads...

> 'XYZ Chartered Accountants. Specialising in helping start-ups get their businesses running quickly, profitably and effectively.'

Which firm of accountants are they likely to choose? The answer is obvious. If you can create this bond between the business and the target market(s) we guarantee you'll grow your firm quicker than you could ever imagine.

Go After The Low-Hanging Fruit

Above all else it is absolutely critical you go for the 'low-hanging fruit' (the easiest businesses to acquire).

For example, if your firm currently has a majority of businesses with a turnover of £100k to £500k you SHOULD NOT be targeting £2m + businesses. Not right now anyway.

We also know that the closer the business is to you (in terms of location) – the more likely they are to use you. So start targeting the businesses closest to you and work outwards.

So how do you target the low-hanging fruit? Well we've created a very simple diagram showing the key characteristics you should look for...

THE TARGET MARKET CHARACTERISTICS

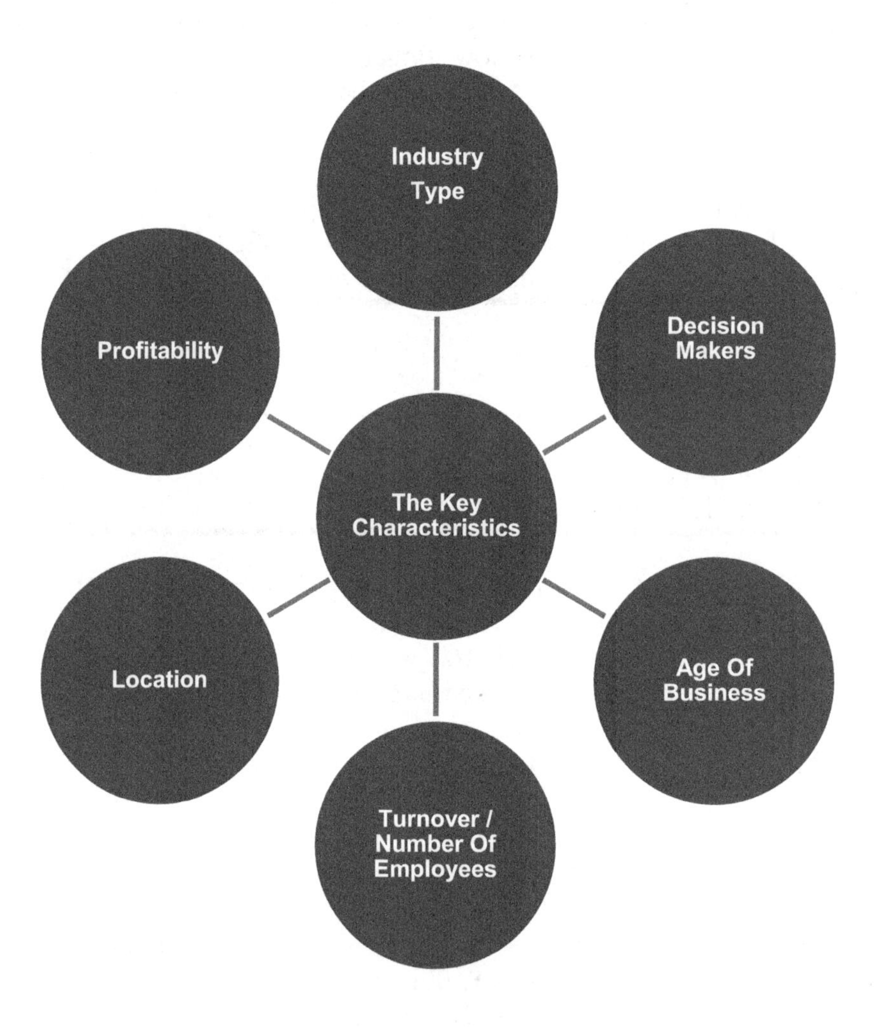

Here's a more in-depth look at each characteristic...

4. How Do We Acquire The Right Clients For Us?

- Industry:

  What types of businesses do you want to target? Are there some industries that you want to stay clear of? Do you have any specialities with certain industries? Do you have credibility in any industries?

  There are three key factors which influence the selection of the industry...

  1. Your industry experience

     You may want to target industries where you already have experience.

  2. Your industry credibility

     You may want to target industries where you already have credibility.

  3. Your likes and dislikes

     You may have preferences already about industries that you like or dislike. This will obviously have an impact on the choices you make in terms of the industries you select.

- Decision Makers:

  An important consideration is choosing businesses with a simple decision-making process. Clearly the larger the business the more likely the number of decision-makers increases, making the sale more difficult.

- Age Of Business:

  Clearly there is an age range of businesses from start-ups to well-established companies. Are you bothered about how old a business is?

- Turnover / Number Of Employees:

  Both these demographics are easy indicators for choosing your target market.

  Turnover has a direct impact on the number of decision-makers and other accounting issues such as the requirement of an audit, etc.

  The Number Of Employees is generally linked to turnover and, again, the greater numbers of staff the larger the company is likely to be. It brings in the decision about working with sole practitioners or not!

  The key here though is to make sure you go after the 'low-hanging fruit'.

  DO NOT TRY AND TARGET LARGER FIRMS THAN YOU'RE CURRENTLY SET UP TO SERVICE IN THE HOPE YOU WILL ACQUIRE THEM.

- Location:

  Since proximity is often a very important part of the decision-making process for many business owners when choosing their accountant, you should start with businesses closest to you and work outwards.

- Profitability:

  How concerned are you about working with profitable companies?

BLACK & GREY ACCOUNTANTS

This is not a time to rush into making knee-jerk and quick decisions about who is the right type of client. Unfortunately Black & Grey do just that.

4. How Do We Acquire The Right Clients For Us?

Of course they have an appreciation of some of the characteristics (namely, size and location), but this is where the biggest mistakes are made.

You see, they fall into the same trap as 80% of other firms and decide that they are going after the types of clients they 'wish' they could work with. In other words, they agree to target companies just under the audit threshold, those with a turnover of £2m-£5m. After all they have a dozen or so clients of this size and they want more.

But if they'd only spent more time on this they'd have researched their existing client base and realised that the majority of their business clients, which generate 60% of their GRFs, have a turnover of £250,000 to £750,000. These are their 'bread and butter' clients. Whether they like it or not, these are the firms that they are good at working with. These are the clients that for whatever reason they are good at acquiring and servicing. These are their low-hanging fruit.

They would also know, if they took the time to analyse, that the average fee for these clients, even though it could be improved (see later), is still a healthy £1,750. Now they may argue that these aren't the right clients for them but, if that's the case, they have to take small steps. It's no good jumping from a target market of £250,000 to £750,000 to a target market of £2m-£5m. Those potential clients are significantly harder to acquire especially when the firm doesn't predominantly work with these types of businesses.

We're not saying you can't have success making these big quantum jumps, but it's very hard and your returns will most likely be poor. It's no different trying to sell sand to the Arabs. Most won't even bother talking to you, but you may get lucky every once in a while!

AFG ACCOUNTANTS LLP

"Do you see, by using the Target Market Characteristics and carefully analysing your existing clients, how you can pinpoint with a fair degree of accuracy who your best target market(s) are?

"Remember, you can make it easy or hard on yourself. If your goal is to work with larger clients (than you're working with right now) then it's much better to steadily increase the size of business you're targeting over a couple of years than it is to try and go after them now.

"Our philosophy is clear: it's far less risky to go after the low-hanging fruit as you steadily build your practice. This way you get the best of both worlds: steady growth and the eventual acquisition of the clients you really want.

"One thing perhaps we haven't made clear just yet is the fact that the larger businesses, £3m plus, have some distinct negatives in trying to work with them.

"First, they most likely have someone in the company responsible for finance. That could be a bookkeeper, or more likely a Financial Controller or Financial Director. As a consequence a number of the value-added services you provide will not be taken up. In other words, it's much harder to sell more to the larger companies because they need you less.

"Second, the larger businesses are harder to sell to. Why? Because the larger the company – the more decision-makers are involved. That just makes your task of acquiring them as clients much harder.

"Third, there are far less businesses with a turnover of over £3m, therefore competition with other firms (usually the larger accountancy firms) is greater, again making it much harder for you to acquire them.

"Yes, a good argument against the larger accountancy firm is a smaller firm can give them a more 'personal service' (whatever that means), but this is all about how you make it easy on yourself. Going after the larger businesses is challenging. Do you really want that challenge when your goal is to grow your firm quickly and easily?

"Look, we're not saying if a larger business comes knocking on your door to turn them away. Of course you go for it. That will almost certainly happen, especially when you start using the strategies we're highlighting here, but we're talking about you creating your own list of businesses that you're going to target (which costs money – unfortunately). So you want to get the maximum return for your investment, in time and money, in the quickest time possible. And this is how you do it.

"Of course before you nail your target market you need to analyse your existing client base. We don't need to make this decision today. So here's what you need to do."

KEY SUMMARY & ACTION POINTS

1. Defining your target market is THE most important thing you can do to grow your practice.
2. Your target market should represent the 'low-hanging fruit' (easy to acquire).
3. Don't try and target clients who are significantly larger (or smaller) than your main group of existing clients who generate a large proportion of your GRFs.

Agenda Item 5

5. How Do We Get People Interested, Even Excited In Our Services?

Introduction

Having identified your target market, you now need to create the message that you are going to deliver to the market.

This isn't a particularly strong area for many businesses including accountancy firms. Our experience tells us that most people really struggle when it comes to creating a powerful message. **THIS IS CERTAINLY A MAJOR REASON WHY MOST MARKETING FAILS.**

Therefore, we will give you a clear insight into why it is so important to create the right message and how to do it.

During the last 20 years or so we've discovered there are a number of crucial elements to a marketing message that, when used correctly, GUARANTEE success.

We call these elements the **'Marketing Assets'**. They are the things that ensure you get a response to your marketing pieces.

So let's take a look at each of the Marketing Assets...

The Marketing Assets	
1	Gaining Competitive Advantage: Unique Perceived Benefit
2	Adding Sizzle To The Steak: Features Into Benefits
3	Irresistible Offers
4	Headlines
5	Guarantees/Risk Reversal
6	Sales Barrier Demolition Strategy
7	Reasons Why
8	Social Proof
9	Call To Action

1. GAINING COMPETITIVE ADVANTAGE: UNIQUE PERCEIVED BENEFIT

A Unique Perceived Benefit (UPB) is the one thing that sets you apart from the competition. Communicating this uniqueness is a powerful and persuasive part of each marketing piece.

This is a very weak area for almost every accountancy firm and one which really hinders growth. As an accountant you will be familiar with the situation where you are sitting opposite a potential client. They have been critical of their current accountant and receptive to everything you say... yet they still won't change. Frustrating!

The problem is that clients (as we said earlier) have become more discerning which means they're looking for reasons to change – unique reasons; competitive advantages; things that are desirable to them that no other firm can offer them.

But because so few firms create this uniqueness most business owners (rightly or wrongly) think ALL accountants are the same. Changing, for the sake of changing, to another accountant who is just going to be like the existing one, just isn't worth the hassle. Better the devil you know!

We have identified 10 proven and powerful different UPB categories. You will be able to choose at least one of them for your business...

1. **New and Unique**

   Sometimes you can provide a service that is so new and unique that the service itself is the UPB. Being the original or first mover in the market is a UPB that nobody can duplicate.

   Inevitably, a competitor will emerge with a knock-off or copy of your service but, until then, you can promote the newness and uniqueness of your service as the UPB.

   When the competition heats up, you can switch your UPB so that it positions your practice as the 'first' or 'original' one of its kind.

   At first thought it can appear impossible to come up with something new in the accountancy market, but this is about coming up with something new and unique that your clients really want. Think laterally.

   For instance, you create a service offering Commercial Awareness training for clients' workforces or you team up with a client to provide Driver Training skills.

2. **Highest Quality**

   One well-known brand that immediately comes to mind when you think about quality is the leading international watch maker, Rolex. Rolex has a short UPB statement that communicates volumes...

   Rolex – "Quality Takes Time"

Rolex have educated the market as to what quality actually means in the context of a watch, and the same is required for clients when it comes to understanding what a 'quality' accountancy firm is. Case studies and testimonials are key and we cover these later.

3. **Expert Status**

This type of UPB communicates the idea that "I/We am/are the top in my/our field. You can trust my/our knowledge and experience".

This works very well for accountants because it can be firmly focused on the target market you have identified. The problem is that few accountants actually market the value of their qualifications and experience.

4. **Amazing Customer Service**

Providing superior customer service is a wonderful way to add value, as well as develop long-term client loyalty.

To surpass the competition you must go beyond simply satisfying customers, you have to AMAZE them.

One of the ways to do this is by using 'Moments Of Truth' (covered later) whereby you look at every point of contact with your clients and create a WOW experience at each point. Think how many times, and in how many different contexts, your firm meets, writes to and telephones clients. This is a huge opportunity going to waste in most firms, not only to impress the client, but to give the client a much better understanding of the true value of the service that they receive.

5. **The Largest Size/Selection**

Providing the largest selection of items can be a powerfully effective UPB. The classic example of this is Amazon.com. For years (prior to extending their product line) Amazon's UPB was “Earth's Biggest Bookstore”.

Even though they were not the first and today they have intense competition, from both online and brick-and-mortar bookstores such as Barnes and Noble and Waterstones, Amazon.com still leads the pack in online bookselling. This is because they clearly differentiated themselves early on by being the biggest.

Accountants are regularly guilty of not communicating to their clients everything that they do. The firms that do this well differentiate themselves as well as sell more.

6. **Speed**

The speed at which your service is delivered can be a powerful UPB.

For example, Regus, the serviced office specialists, have a very powerful 3-word UPB that sums up their uniqueness perfectly (quick and everywhere)...

“Instant Offices Worldwide”

FedEx changed the shipping world when it began guaranteeing overnight delivery of packages. Their UPB has stood the test of time...

FedEx – “When It Absolutely Has To Be There Overnight”

One of the most common frustrations quoted by businesses about their accountant is that tasks take too long. The firm that addresses this and then markets it takes a step forward over the competition.

7. Strongest Guarantee/Risk Reversal/Sales Barrier Demolition

A powerful guarantee/risk reversal/sales barrier demolition can immediately give you a compelling UPB.

Craftsman Tools is a prime example of this UPB category. Like all carefully crafted UPBs the Craftsman statement leaves you with no doubt as to what their main advantage is...

Craftsman Tools – "Hand tools so tough, they're guaranteed forever"

Guarantees are creeping into the profession. For example...

"Your accounts done within six weeks or they are FREE!"

As a professional, systemised firm, guarantees should be matter of fact. The key is therefore to find ones that are meaningful and stand out in your market place. What is it that will reassure your target market?

8. Problem/Solution

Understand that you are not selling a service, you're selling a major solution to your target market's most pressing problem(s). Think about the following situation...

You're out for a business lunch and someone you've been speaking to asks you this very familiar question...

"What do you do for a living?"

Now, when the same question is put to you, you probably answer in this way...

"I'm an accountant"

5. How Do We Get People Interested In Our Services?

This is a very common reply and most people will 'switch off' after asking this question and hearing that reply!

What you must realise is that when you answer in this way regarding your own business, you're saying what you ARE, rather than what you DO FOR YOUR CLIENTS!

There's a massive difference.

The good news is your competition ALSO answer in this way – they don't have a UPB. All they are selling is the 'service' and not the result!

To show you what we mean, let's take two common examples and add a UPB...

> Solicitor – "I help people separate within 12 weeks and as amicably as possible"
>
> Printer – "I help people sell more of their products or services using innovative and cost-effective printed materials"

In essence, your UPB completely focuses on what you do for your specific target market(s) or niche(s). It is the major benefit to them – the result of using your services.

By focusing on the customer's most pressing problems you can uncover the major benefit.

Think about your prospects' and clients' fears, obstacles and problems. How does your service reduce or eliminate these fears? For example, a telemarketing service company would say the major problem their prospects and clients have is...

They can't generate enough leads or enquiries themselves.

Here's how you'd then turn this problem into a powerful benefit...

Problem: They can't generate any leads or enquiries.

Benefit: We help businesses generate high-quality leads.

Do you see how easy this is?

So having identified the major problem your service solves for your chosen target market(s), write the corresponding benefit down. For example:

Problem (start-ups): They don't know what they should be doing.

Benefit: We help start-up businesses by guiding them through the business jungle.

Problem (owner-managers): They don't have enough hours in a day.

Benefit: We help businesses free up time by taking over their compliance and back-office tasks.

If you have identified two or more target markets, it is highly likely you will have one UPB for each target market (which are likely to be different from each other).

9. Magic Wand

If you could wave a magic wand and give your clients and target market(s) one wish, what would they want most?

Some of the greatest businesses in the world were founded on such thinking. For example, Microsoft was built on this premise...

"to make the computer accessible and easy-to-use for everyone"

In an inexpensive way, can you reposition your basic offer in order to meet the target market's major need?

5. How Do We Get People Interested In Our Services?

How about this for a firm whose target market is small, owner-managed businesses:

> "To support your business in everything that you do, making life easier, less risky and more profitable"

10. THE Biggest, Most Important Benefit

This final method is relatively simple. You need to identify every single feature of your service, together with how you operate as a firm and how you interact with your clients. Having written them down, you then need to convert each of these features into benefits (see the next section on how to do this).

Once you have your list of benefits, you then need to put them in order, with the most potent one at the top. If this is powerful then the major benefit of the service will be the UPB.

A good example of this is the 'Tech-ni-fold Tri-Creaser'. The major benefit of the Tri-creaser is that it 'totally eliminates fibre-cracking'. This benefit on its own is so powerful it became the UPB. It was further strengthened by adding the word 'guaranteed' to it...

"Totally Eliminates Fibre-Cracking – Guaranteed"

Now to you and us this means very little, but to printers and print finishers this means everything!

Let's give you an example closer to home...

> "Our systemised, guaranteed self-assessment tax return service totally removes the risk of you receiving a late filing penalty from the taxman"

A VERY IMPORTANT NOTE ABOUT USING THE LOWEST PRICE AS THE UPB –

NEVER, EVER DO IT

Guaranteeing the lowest price has been used as a UPB for many businesses and right now, a large number of accountancy firms are trying to 'buy' clients in this way.

However, cutting profit margins too deeply is rarely healthy for a business. So, unfortunately, many who have chosen low price for a UPB are no longer in business or are struggling to make ends meet. The philosophy is low margins, but high volume. This is a very difficult model to adopt successfully for a firm of accountants.

We NEVER recommend setting your stall out to be the cheapest. There is always someone who will undercut you. So-called "low balling" is one of the main reasons why business people don't value the services of an accountant. Why would you value a product where each supplier simply sets out to be cheaper than the last one?

2. ADDING SIZZLE TO THE STEAK: FEATURES INTO BENEFITS

A 'Feature' is a statement of what you do or what something does. It has limited value as it doesn't communicate the 'what's in it for me' factor that all buyers are looking for.

A 'Benefit' is the opposite of a feature. It communicates the end result that the buyer could expect to receive, i.e. something they get rather than something you do. It's amazing how many marketing pieces we see, especially from accountants, with more features than benefits.

5. How Do We Get People Interested In Our Services?

Look at the most obvious. The majority of accountants' marketing pieces still list the fact that the firm does "accounts and tax". This is rather like a plumber announcing that he fixes pipes – we all know that, hence why we look for a plumber when we need our pipes fixing. How much more effective if the accountant's advert talked about "completely removing the accounts and tax compliance burden from your business...and an end to penalties".

3. Irresistible Offers

This is the part of your marketing that makes someone choose to take action or not. In other words, the offer is what the client actually gets when they buy from you. An irresistible offer can transform the success of a marketing campaign.

Any offer can be improved by using the following 'Offer Equation'...

Great Offer = Irresistible Promotion + Stimulator (getting people to act now, i.e. a deadline, limited availability, etc.).

Again, let's put this into the context of a basic service...

> "£100 off the price of your tax return every year if you let us have your papers by the 30th September"

4. Headline

A marketing piece without a headline is a mistake made by 95% of businesses, and yet the headline is the 'ad for the ad'. Your firm's name, for example, is NOT a headline.

Unfortunately people don't care about the name of your firm – all they care about is what you can do for them. The headline is the one thing that grabs their attention. Like all of these Marketing Assets, a powerful headline is absolutely compulsory!

A headline we have used very successfully is...

"Don't Contact Another Accountant
Until You've Read This"

5. GUARANTEE

As we highlighted above when discussing UPB, a guarantee is a proven way to reduce 'buyer hurdles' and is therefore a 'sales converter'. In other words, by offering a guarantee, you eliminate doubts in the mind of the potential client, resulting in more new clients.

Guaranteeing things like fixed fees, work completed on time, response times, and so on can make a huge difference to you.

6. SALES BARRIER DEMOLITION

This takes the concept of guarantees to another level. By focusing on the fears and frustrations your clients have with the accountancy industry as a whole, you can create a multi-step guarantee (Sales Barrier Demolition) which completely obliterates any buyer hurdles, significantly increasing sales.

For example, offering a 'FREE Telephone Advice Hotline' that clients can use at any time, eliminates the fear most people have that they're 'on the clock' as soon as they speak with you. In these competitive times you have to take this even further and it has to be clear and unequivocal. The guarantee shown below totally removes any client fear that prevents them from contacting you...

"We agree an annual price with you and absolutely promise you that there will be no more charges in the year for the agreed package. All phone calls, e-mails, letters and meetings are included...as often as you like, on any subject you like. Talk to us, come in and see us as often as you want at no extra cost whatsoever."

Please note, on first inspection of this you may think this will be a cost to the firm; however, operated correctly, it is a great way to increase fees. Clients are busy people too. One in a hundred may abuse it but the other ninety-nine make the whole approach very worthwhile.

7. Reasons Why

When you have an irresistible offer and a guarantee, you must use 'Reasons Why' to explain why you're offering these things. This ensures the potential customer believes your claims and further increases new client acquisitions.

> "Why do we offer you unlimited free meetings and phone calls? Because we know that you talking to us sooner rather than later is better for both our businesses. You get advice and support at the right time, resulting in fewer problems for us to sort out later."

8. Social Proof

Social Proof is a combination of assets which help prove your credentials, resulting in more sales. Here's a list of the things we class as Social Proof ...

- Quotes/testimonials from happy clients
- Awards of any kind
- Membership of credible associations ('credible' in the mind of the prospect/client)
- Review quotes from other media sources
- Quotes from business partners
- Any mention of a joint venture with a well-known brand
- Singing your praises from the rooftops (or more conveniently in your reception area) is a good thing and an

easy opportunity for most firms. Yet it's missed time and time again.

9. CALL TO ACTION

This is an essential part of the marketing piece and a critical Marketing Asset.

The 'Call To Action' needs to give the reader a reason to ACT NOW, e.g. a FREE phone number is not a call to action, a reduced fee for responding by a certain date, is. Ideally it should (1) summarise the offer, (2) remind them of the 'stimulator', (3) give them multiple ways of responding and (4) tell them what will happen when they respond/buy.

BLACK & GREY ACCOUNTANTS

Getting the message right is a significant weakness for Black & Grey. Lack of expertise in this area means the message that Black & Grey will convey to their target market will be weak.

They are again not alone! This is a breakdown of what will be included (or not included) as part of their overall message...

1. Unique Perceived Benefit

They agree that fixed price quotes are their uniqueness.

At least they've tried to hang their hat on something.

But although many firms do not adopt this approach (even though they should), this is not uniqueness. Unfortunately Black & Grey believe it is enough to do the job of a UPB. It isn't!

They also believe that saying things like 'proactive', 'personal service', 'value', 'reliability', 'support', 'service second to none' 'save tax' and 'maximise profits' will strike a chord with potential clients. Again they're wrong – very wrong. We call the use of these vague statements 'puffery'. Any firm can say these things (and most do) so none of this sets the firm apart from the competition.

And, more importantly, none of it makes the potential client sit up and think – wow!

Furthermore, they believe they should always list the services they provide. Again this is a common practice adopted by most firms. For example, here's an extensive list of commonly used terms (and in no particular order)...

- Business Planning
- Raising Finance
- Profit Improvement
- Tax Advice
- Accountancy Services
- Bookkeeping & Payroll
- Audit & Accountancy
- VAT & Income Tax Advice
- Start-Ups
- Self-Employed
- Partnerships
- Limited Companies
- Self-Assessment
- Support Services
- Personal Tax

You have to think about this logically. It's like seeing an ad for a butcher saying 'we do all kinds of meat'. You're just stating the obvious – and none of it is compelling.

Clients and potential clients expect all these things as standard. The only time you should mention a particular service is if it is genuinely unique and one that will help you generate interest. Otherwise you are wasting your time. A list of services DOES NOT WORK in attracting people to your firm and DOES NOT POSITION YOU DIFFERENTLY FROM EVERY OTHER FIRM!

2. Features Into Benefits

It's always interesting to look in the Yellow Pages and review what each firm lists as benefits. Do it yourself now. Turn to the accountancy category and look at each ad. What benefits are listed? Do you see any?

For example, a list of 'services' is NOT a list of benefits. The fact that you work with 'start-ups' is not a benefit. A 'Free no-obligation meeting' is not a benefit. 'Fixed Fees' is not a benefit.

Now since Black & Grey are constructing their uniqueness around 'Fixed Fees' (they genuinely believe this is a UPB) – they are currently simply stating the feature.

The benefit for this feature would be something like...

"You know to the penny how much you will pay for our services. There are never any nasty shocks. You can budget accordingly and relax in the knowledge that your fees are fixed at the start of each year."

Look at the difference between this and just saying 'fixed fees'. You've transformed a dull, one-dimensional feature into a more exciting emotional appeal.

3. Irresistible Offer

We can't get around the fact that you want to meet with potential clients. As we said earlier, a 'Free No-Obligation Meeting' in itself isn't a benefit, but it is an offer.

Black & Grey are going to persist in offering this as their key offer.

But remember, EVERY firm offers this. It's like personal injury solicitors making a big deal out of 'no win, no fee'. Because everyone offers this you have to change it, add something to it, or add some kind of value to it. Otherwise the potential client will not be moved to do anything.

4. Headline

Since Black & Grey don't understand the importance of having a compelling headline as part of the message, they do what 80% of firms do, and simply use the name of the firm.

If you don't believe us, look back at your Yellow Pages and count how many ads have weak, meaningless or clever headlines, or the name of the firm as the headline.

No matter how long your firm has been operating, and no matter how successful it is – the name of your firm will never grab the attention of a prospective client as much as a powerful headline. Leading with the firm's name is a sure way to reduce your marketing to zero effectiveness. You've been warned!

5. Guarantee

Black & Grey do not know the value of guarantees or why they should even use them. They offer good levels of service – so why bother?

The point is, however, that guarantees, in the mind of the prospective client, demonstrate that you stand behind everything you do. Remember, until they start using you (and usually for many months or years later), a client won't know how good you are as accountants. Your services are in the main intangible.

If you can reassure the prospective client that you have a strong guarantee which demonstrates to them that you DO deliver on your promises, then this is one more reason why they should choose you over and above any other firm.

6. Sales Barrier Demolition

Black & Grey aren't even aware of this (nor would they be – it's something we have created, that's unique to us).

7. Reasons Why

Since Black & Grey don't have any real irresistible offers or startling guarantees then, even though they aren't aware of the importance of reasons why, their message will be devoid of any.

8. Social Proof

The good news is that Black & Grey do use testimonials (two). They do understand their importance and they will be part of their message. Unfortunately they've committed a common mistake and presented their testimonials in a way which achieves the opposite of what they should do (build credibility). For example, here's how they present each testimonial...

> "I have used Black & Grey for over five years on a business and personal basis. Their professionalism and competence in handling my affairs has been exemplary. They adopt a 'can-do' attitude and are prepared to go the extra mile to satisfy a client. Having used large national accountancy firms in the past, the level of service I receive from Black & Grey is most gratifying and I know the answer to any query I have is only a telephone call away. I have no hesitation in recommending them to anyone seeking a caring, personal and professional service. Nice people to do business with and they make life much less taxing!"
>
> *AS - Stourbridge*

Can you see what's wrong with this?

The testimonial itself is actually quite good. It could be better with more actual specifics ("They've helped us grow the business from £540k to £1.2m", etc.) but it builds credibility and highlights a number of valuable attributes.

5. How Do We Get People Interested In Our Services?

Unfortunately Black & Grey, for some reason, have reduced the full name to just initials and omitted the company name.

This is very common. And it's a big mistake.

This renders the testimonial meaningless and in fact can do the firm more harm than good. By choosing to omit the actual source of the testimonial, the potential client doesn't believe it, or at least doubts its authenticity.

The firm are also members of the ACCA and the ICAEW so will use these to add credibility, which is a wise decision.

9. Call To Action

Black & Grey don't realise how important the Call To Action is, so their marketing pieces and their message won't include a powerful one. Instead they will just mention the phone number and possibly their web address.

AFG Accountants LLP

"So once you've settled on your target market the message you convey to them is all-important. Most people don't realise that for a message to compel a prospective client to respond to you, it needs these nine Marketing Assets.

"But it's not just about including them in your message. It's also about making sure they are included correctly. How you do it is as important as what you do.

"So let's take a look at how to ensure the Marketing Assets combine to give you a compelling message.

"Now at the moment you suffer from the same affliction as most other firms, in that you don't have a uniqueness. You don't differentiate your firm from the competition.

"This, although right now you may not think so, has serious consequences. You see, not being seen as being different not only makes it harder for you to acquire clients – it makes their decision-making harder too and leads them to one horrible but common conclusion on the only way they can choose you over and above other firms.

"So to make you understand this further, let's just go through the following scenario.

"Let's turn the tables and say you're running a business and you're looking for a new accountant. So you ask your friends if they can recommend a good one, but none of them can. So where would you go to find an accountant?

"That's right, either the internet or the Yellow Pages. But let's say you choose the internet.

"You type into Google 'accountant in Leicester' and dozens of firms are listed. You then systematically start clicking on each firm to have a look at them to see which one jumps out at you. But it's not easy for you to choose who to contact. Is it?

"Why?

"That's right, because all the websites say the same things. None of the firms differentiate. None of the firms target your type of business as a key target market. Everyone is just listing their services. No one is saying choose us, we're different because…!

"Now you have a dilemma. How do you choose the three firms you're going to call to hopefully meet with?

"It's not easy, but you use what seems to be a logical process. You choose three firms that are closest to you and seem to 'look' like they are professional and can deal with you and your business. You don't know you're doing this, but you also look for clues on who would be the best firm to work with. These clues are the Marketing Assets, such as headlines, testimonials, guarantees and the like. But whilst the three firms you've chosen seem to be the best, none of them actually provide compelling reasons for you to get in touch. But this doesn't perturb you. You've managed to whittle your list down to three firms. Now you're ready to call them.

"You call each firm with a view to making an appointment. In fairness all three companies handle the call equally well and you make an appointment to meet with all three accountants.

"Then you meet with each one and, although all of them seem to know what they're talking about, no one really tells you why you should use their accounting services. Why they're different. Why they're better for you than any other firm.

"Does this sound familiar?

"They all say they'll write to you confirming what their fees are. They'll send you a quote.

"You now eagerly await the quotes. And as promised, they all arrive a couple of days after the meeting. Yet again the quotes all look the same, with one difference – the price is different on each quote. (See a typical example of a quotation on the following page.)

"Remember, none of these firms have taken the time or made the effort to differentiate themselves. And that's the dilemma faced by you – the prospective client. You see, because you believe all the firms are the SAME you now have just one justifiable and real way to differentiate between all three firms.

"Any idea?

"Yes, that's right – PRICE.

"Because no firm has differentiated themselves, the only way the prospect can make a decision is based on price. That doesn't necessarily mean they choose the lowest price (more on this later), but it creates an artificial situation where the accountants (and the industry at large) believe that price is becoming THE significant factor when choosing an accountant. Price of course plays a part in all purchasing decisions (more so for a small percentage of people who always buy the cheapest) but when you don't differentiate, you force the prospective client down the price route – which ISN'T THEIR FAULT."

A TYPICAL QUOTATION – HOW NOT TO DO IT

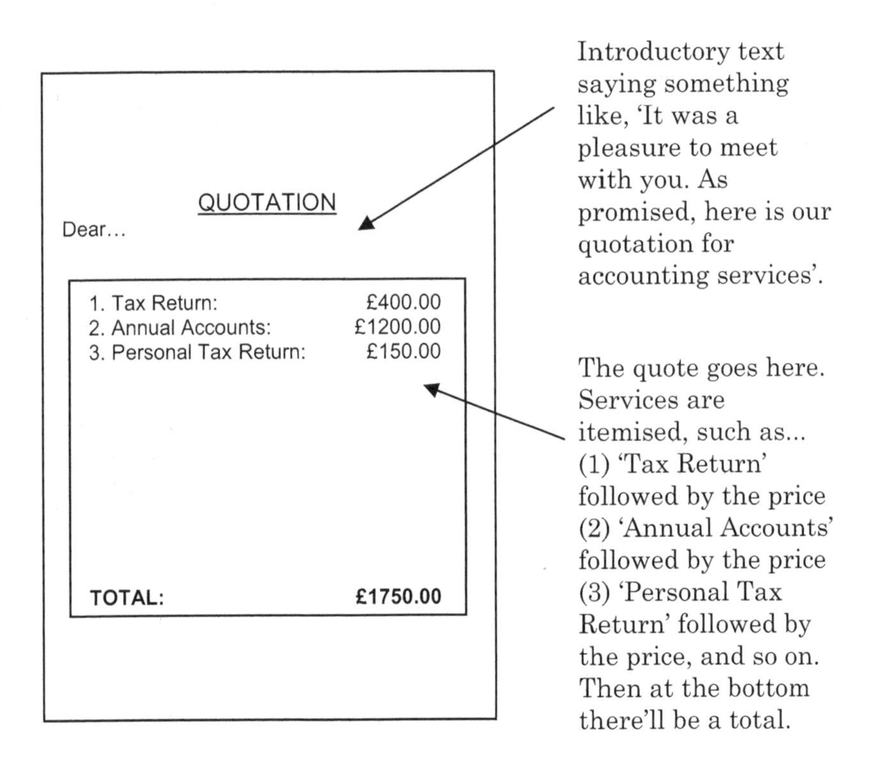

"It's YOUR fault. So now when you think your market seems to be price-sensitive or you feel under pressure with fees, you understand why, and in many cases this can be avoided simply by differentiating your firm from every other firm.

"This becomes more powerful when your differentiation is focused on your identified target market(s) and you are giving them something they genuinely desire. This is the secret to differentiation: give the target market something they highly desire that no other firm can offer. Do that and you have the makings of a message that will be magnetic to your target market.

5. How Do We Get People Interested In Our Services?

"We've given you the 10 methods for creating your uniqueness. What you need to think about now is what could you focus on that will be highly attractive to your target market and at the same time be difficult for your competition to copy or exploit.

"That takes us nicely on to benefits. These are the things that add 'sizzle to the steak'. Just because you're running a firm of accountants, it doesn't mean you have to be boring. Your benefits should leap out at the target market and reinforce to them that you are the firm to go to. Of course the more relevant and meaningful the benefits are to your target market – the more importance they will have.

"So you've now got a UPB and a set of benefits that are focused on your target market. Are you starting to see why choosing the right target market(s) in the first place is so important? What you're doing is creating a message that is so laser-focused on the target market that, when your message is delivered to them, you're making it very hard for the recipient to say 'no'. This is target marketing at its best.

"Next is your offer. Now as we said earlier we can't get away from the fact that ultimately you're going to be offering a free no-obligation meeting. But there's so much you can do to make your offer much more appealing then any other firm.

"The first question to ask yourself when trying to craft an irresistible offer is: 'What can I offer that positions me as an expert and at the same time is desirable for my target market?'

"You have to forget about the meeting for a second to be able to do this. Let us put it another way... what can you give your target market that makes them think 'wow, this firm is a real expert in my field'?

"By far and away the best thing you can do that adds enormous credibility, and positions you as an expert with your target market, is to create a publication. This can take the form of a number of things, from a printed book to special reports and articles. A book of course gives you the ultimate credibility but articles, and special reports in particular, can achieve similar results. For example, let's say your target market is based on businesses with a turnover of £250k to £750k. Your special report could be entitled 'Breaking Through The £1m A Year Barrier: 17 Little Known Financial & Business Growth Strategies That Get You There Quicker'. Now, to a business owner who is turning over, say, £500k, this report is irresistible. You now have the makings of something very powerful to give as part of your overall offer.

"Your report can have any title as long as it clearly identifies the target market you're seeking. You'll offer your report as part of the incentive for a potential client to meet with you. You're already starting to move away from the competition when it comes to the offer. Here's how you take it to the next level.

"Since everyone else is offering a 'free meeting', you need to do something different that again makes meeting with you more favourable then meeting with anyone else. You do this by explaining in simple terms WHY giving up 90 minutes of their time will be so valuable to them. Tell them that during the meeting you'll be able to give them 2 or 3 pearls of wisdom about their business that they never knew and they can take away with them. Tell them that because you work with their type of businesses day in, day out, you know how they tick and you can give them tips that will improve their cash flow, their profitability and simultaneously help them to save more tax. You do this automatically anyway (you're good accountants), but telling them this up-front makes a huge difference to their decision-making process.

"The final piece of the jigsaw really sets you apart. Tell them that if they don't think this is the most worthwhile meeting they've had in the last 12 months, you'll write a cheque for £200 made out to their favourite charity. Now you're guaranteeing the meeting will be of immense value and indirectly you're putting a cost on their time.

"We then complete the offer equation by clearly stating that your free special report, worth £97, is only available for free during the next 21 days. This is your 'stimulator'. You use this to reduce procrastination.

"So now you have an irresistible offer. You've got a report which adds credibility and positions you as an expert. You have several reasons why the meeting will be so worthwhile. You have a guarantee and you have a stimulator. Compare that to the norm. Compare that to Black & Grey who like every other firm are simply offering a 'no-obligation meeting'. Who would you rather meet, and we're only a third of the way towards completing your message? This is very powerful stuff.

"Next, the headlines you use need to grab attention. We've explained that the headline is one of the most important elements of the message because it forces the recipient to read/listen to or watch what you have to say. A poor headline means no matter how good your message, the target market will simply pass you by. Think of it like you're waiting for a bus to stop. You can wait by a proper bus stop (the headline) and 99 times out of 100 the bus will stop and let you on. Or you can take your chances and stand anywhere in the street, hold your hand out and hope the bus will stop. You might get lucky 5 times in every 100. That's the difference between a good and a bad headline.

"And like everything else, your headline needs to connect with the target market. So, if your target market is 'start-ups', then a headline such as 'Attention Start-Ups: How You Too Can Create A Thriving Business' will attract more attention with the target market than a more general headline 'How You Too Can Create A Thriving Business'. Compare these two to the headline 'Black & Grey'.

"When you see it like this, hopefully you can immediately understand why the headline plays such an important role, and why the name of your firm really is the worst headline you could ever use!

"If prospects or customers dismiss the headline – that's it, you've lost them. They won't start reading your letter, ad, brochure, etc., or listening to your telephone script or radio ad – and you won't get a response or a sale.

"To emphasise the importance of headlines, here are a couple of quotes from two of the most highly respected copywriters of all time...

> **"If you can come up with a good headline, you are almost sure to have a good ad. But even the greatest writer can't save an ad with a poor headline."**
>
> John Caples - How To Make Your Advertising Make Money
>
> **"On average five times as many people read the headline as read the body copy."**
>
> David Ogilvy - Confessions Of An Advertising Man

"What does this mean? Basically, if you get your headline right you almost guarantee your success. Get your headline wrong - and your results will suffer!

"Here's a simple example to show how few people understand the basic principle of using headlines...

"We've just picked up a copy of the Yellow Pages directory. We're looking in the Accountancy category. These are the 'headlines' of the ads on one page:

- Pearson Jones
- Powlett & Smith
- R Graham & Co
- Richard Prentice Partnership
- Sturgeon Simpson & Co

- Shappleton Accountants

- Shardrake Fellows

- S.R. Connaught

- Running your own business

"With the exception of the last headline, the headline for each ad is the name of the business that's advertising.

"Because so many people are doing it wrong, if all you do is lead with a strong headline on all your marketing communications, you'll improve the response and success many times over.

Effective Headlines Fulfil These Four Key Objectives...

- Get attention
- Select an audience
- Deliver a complete message
- Draw the reader into the body copy (or keep them listening to you, etc.)

"The good news is that creating winning headlines can be achieved by following some simple and proven 'headline types'. We've listed seven of the most successful ones here. By applying a number of these different headline types you'll start to see how you can create winning headlines...

- **Benefit headlines** (all your headlines should contain a benefit of some sort)

- **Use a two- or three-word headline (**but remember long headlines are almost always more successful then short headlines)

- Get One Month Free
- Double Bonus Service
- Oh My God!
- Gosh
- At Last
- Millionaire Secrets
- If Only...

- **Headlines that focus on quick and easy solutions**

    - Fast And Simple...
    - Ridiculously Easy And Fast...
    - Idiot-Proof...
    - In Just 10 Days...
    - The 7-Minute Workout...
    - The Lazy Man's Way To...
    - Instant, Automatic Results...
    - The Quick And Easy Way To...

- **Warning headlines**

    - Read This Before You...
    - Don't Choose Another Accountant Until You've Read These Facts

- **Testimonial headlines**

    - A Specific Benefit Written Testimonial From One Of Your Clients
    - "Or It Can Just Be A Headline In Speech Marks Like This Written Like A Testimonial"

- **Reasons why headlines**

    - Seven Reasons Why You Should...
    - 37 Invigorating Reasons...
    - 6 Ways To...
    - 7 Steps...
    - Here's How...

5. How Do We Get People Interested In Our Services?

- **Offer headlines**

  – Put your offer in the headline…
  – Try-Before-You-Buy Accountancy Service

"Now let's talk about guarantees. Accountants have generally been slow on the take-up of guarantees.

"As you know, the benefit of your service is gained **after** the sale is made. After you have acquired the client. Sometimes this can be days, weeks, months or even years after the first sale was made. This in itself places an enormous risk on the shoulders of would-be clients. It's this risk that often prevents them from buying or moving from one firm to the next – even though they're not happy.

"However, if you lower or eliminate this risk, then the natural consequence is people will be more inclined to buy from you.

"That's the secret of creating a powerful guarantee that reverses the risk.

"A guarantee is nothing more than simply taking away the barriers from the sale and ensures that the prospect keeps progressing towards the sale.

"As soon as you add a guarantee it removes the risks of buying, ensuring more clients are gained. It automatically differentiates the firm from the competition. And it adds value.

"Prospects will value your services much more because they'll assume the service must live up to expectations, and the firm must be excellent at delivering the service ('Why would they offer a guarantee if the product or service wasn't great?').

"The result is therefore a BIG increase in new clients!

"The ultimate aim is to guarantee the result or main benefit of your service and add a 'penalty' should the service fail to live up to your promises.

"Here's how it looks...

Perfect Guarantee	=	Guarantee the result or benefit of your service	+	Penalise your firm if result not achieved

"Just to explain this further, here's a simple example of how risk reversal works. A man wants to buy a puppy for his daughter. He responds to two ads in the local newsagent's window. He examines the first puppy and it seems ideal in temperament and looks. The owner says to the man, 'If the dog isn't right for your daughter, bring it back in one week and I'll give you your money back.' Clearly he appreciated the value of risk reversal but he didn't fully understand it!

"The man then goes to look at the second puppy. Again it seems ideal in temperament and looks. Only this time the owner says, 'Your daughter is obviously looking forward to her new puppy and it's important that she's totally happy with it. Please take the puppy, let your daughter play with it, look after it, and get to know it. If after three weeks the puppy is not right for her, bring the puppy back, and I'll refund your money in full and give you £25 for your time, effort and trouble.'

"Now this man really understands risk reversal. First he extended the 'trial' period. He knows that his puppy is a good dog. He also knows after three weeks the puppy and girl will be inseparable. He totally reverses the risk.

"You also need to understand this. The company that reverses the risk, automatically gains competitive advantage and wins more business – in fact much more! This competitive advantage is very significant when attracting new clients to your firm.

"Here's another example, it's one of the best we've ever seen. It's from a pest control company called BBBK. Their guarantee is aimed at hotels and restaurants but again you can adopt something similar for your own practice.

5. How Do We Get People Interested In Our Services?

> You don't owe one penny until all the pests on your premises have been eradicated...if you are ever dissatisfied with BBBK's services you will receive a refund for up to 12 months of the company's services...plus fees for another exterminator of your choice for the next year.
>
> If a guest spots a pest on your premises, BBBK will pay for the guest's meal or room, send a letter of apology, and pay for a future meal or stay...and if your facility is closed down due to the presence of roaches or rodents, BBBK will pay any fines, as well as all lost profits, plus $5,000.

"Although we don't know for certain, it's easy to **assume** several things about BBBK from this guarantee. They are very good at pest control. They understand the concerns of their customers with regard to hygiene. They are very successful at attracting new customers! They are probably providing very similar services to their competitors. However, they understand risk reversal. Their **profits,** we're sure, will reflect this!

"Let's put this into accountancy terms...

> "We guarantee to deliver all our work to you on time, every time. We agree with you, in advance, a date for completion and if we fail to meet that date, you don't pay a penny. It's absolutely free! What's more, if at any time you are dissatisfied with the quality or level of service that we provide to you then you decide the fee. No arguments, no quibble, you decide what we're worth."

"Hopefully you now have a basic grasp of guarantees and what they can achieve for your practice. If you've given any thought to the strategy, several questions may be entering your mind.

"For example, 'Won't people try to abuse what I am offering?' and 'Won't I lose a lot of money with this?' The key, of course, to successful guarantees is this – if you offer a good service (which you do) then you have nothing to worry about.

"Unfortunately we cannot say no one will ask for a refund or for their money back (or whatever your guarantee states). What we can say is that, for every one of these, you will attract many more prospects and clients by simply offering a guarantee in the first place.

"Your guarantee is usually the one thing that tips the scales in your favour. Because you offer a guarantee, your prospect thinks and assumes the following things about you. First, if you're offering this guarantee, you must be very good at what you do. And second, you would be 'foolish' to offer such a guarantee if you were poor at delivering your promises.

"In the prospect's mind the guarantee has 'proven' to him or her that you can give them exactly what they need. More importantly, when most people choose to buy an accountancy service, they choose it for perfectly good reasons and intentions. And they spend time making their decision. They wouldn't choose you in the first place if they wanted to capitalise on the guarantee.

"Therefore you should be thinking about guaranteeing the services you provide. Guaranteeing delivery times on work. Guaranteeing support services. You name it, whatever you do and how you do it – you can guarantee it, and the bolder you are – the better.

"That takes us nicely onto Sales Barrier Demolition. One guarantee on its own can do wonders for you, but a multi-layered guarantee – or as we prefer to call it, a Sales Barrier Demolition Guarantee – has the ability to take your firm to unprecedented heights. Probably the best way to demonstrate this to you is by taking an example from another industry and show you how powerful a multi-layered guarantee can become.

5. How Do We Get People Interested In Our Services?

"This is the Sales Barrier Demolition for a kitchen replacement company. They don't completely strip out the kitchen. They simple replace the doors, drawers, worktops, sinks, etc., and by doing so give the kitchen a whole new facelift for a fraction of the cost of a brand new kitchen.

"A successful Sales Barrier Demolition Strategy focuses on the pressing fears, worries and frustrations that customers have in terms of the industry at large. So for example, a kitchen replacement company is a contractor, and people have fears such as: they don't start when they say they're going to start; they will leave the job unfinished; they will pay more than they were quoted; they'll leave a mess every day; they won't finish on time, and so on.

"So by focusing on these fears we can create a compelling Sales Barrier Demolition like this.

Our Unrivalled 7-Point Guarantee...

1. We guarantee we'll start when we say we will
2. We guarantee we'll start every morning when we say we will
3. We guarantee we'll leave your kitchen tidy and clean at the end of each day
4. We guarantee we'll never leave your kitchen until we've finished it
5. We guarantee we'll finish your kitchen when we say we will
6. We guarantee your bill will be as quoted – not a penny more
7. We guarantee our products and workmanship for five years

"Now read that again. If you were looking for a kitchen replacement company, don't you think this would be extremely attractive to you? Note, price doesn't come into it!

"Then, to give it extra oomph, you completely reverse the risk so the customer doesn't take any risk should the business NOT deliver on its promises. Instead you're putting the risk on your shoulders (reversing the risk).

"Here's how it's done (the words in bold show you the added elements).

Our Unrivalled 7-Point ***MONEY-BACK*** *Guarantee...*

1. We guarantee we'll start when we say we will
2. We guarantee we'll start every morning when we say we will
3. We guarantee we'll leave your kitchen tidy and clean at the end of each day
4. We guarantee we'll never leave your kitchen until we've finished it
5. We guarantee we'll finish your kitchen when we say we will
6. We guarantee your bill will be as quoted – not a penny more
7. We guarantee our products and workmanship for five years

If we don't deliver on all 7 guarantees 100% of the time – you don't pay us a single penny. In other words, your kitchen is FREE if we 'foul up'.

"When you use a sensational guarantee, offer or sales barrier demolition it is important to back it up with what we call 'Reasons Why'. We require 'reasons why' because, unless you tell people why you offer such things, they can dismiss what you're saying, they think it's too good to be true. So your 'reasons why' validates and makes your message sound believable.

"For example, here's the 'reasons why' that you could have for the sales barrier demolition above.

So why would we do this? Simple. The guarantee states in the open our high level of service. Last year we refurbished 2,314 kitchens. Not one of our customers got their kitchen for free.

That means one thing – we deliver on our promises, and I'm sure you'll agree in our industry this is rare. So for us our guarantee isn't a risk; but for you it delivers complete peace of mind. And that's important – very important.

"Do you see what we're doing here? The 'Reasons Why' actually supports and validates the Sales Barrier Demolition strategy, but, equally as important, it's a very powerful sales tool and marketing asset!

"What further supports your message and proves that you do deliver on your promises is the use of Social Proof. Client testimonials and other credibility builders are key ingredients that add believability.

"We note that you have a couple of testimonials – but once you've identified your target market, you need to get testimonials from other clients that fit the target market.

"Once again it's this tailoring of your message to fit the target market that will help you get big leaps in client acquisitions of the right type of clients. For example, if your target market is businesses who turnover £2m to £5m, the only testimonials you should be using are from businesses of a similar size. We cannot overstate the importance of this. Relevance is a key motivator, so the more relevant everything is to the target market – the more appealing you'll become.

"Furthermore, your testimonials should ideally stress a number of your key benefits. The more positive the reinforcement of your overall offer – the better.

"Now you may think getting client testimonials is challenging. It's not. Simply write to the relevant clients and ask them to give you a few comments about what they like about your services, and ask for their permission to use their comments on your material. You'll be surprised at the responses you get, and how good the comments are.

"Then once you've got your supply of testimonials, simply use the ones which convey your benefits best. It really is that simple!

"And finally we complete our message by using a powerful 'Call To Action'. The purpose of every marketing piece is simple: you must get the recipient to act and you must get them to act now!

"Getting anyone to DO something isn't easy. In fact, responding is usually inconvenient. More often than not the prospect or client is busy. Other things are more important.

"It's very easy for your prospect to say to themselves, 'I'll reply tomorrow.' But as we all know, tomorrow never comes!

"Therefore your number one goal is to get a response now. Your call to action is all-important in achieving this objective. Tests have proved that without a call to action your marketing piece is likely to be 50% less effective – that's how important the Call To Action is.

"As we mentioned earlier, a good Call To Action summarises the offer, explains what the recipient needs to do to act now and includes the stimulator to reduce procrastination.

"Working hard at creating a powerful message by including all the marketing assets will be time very well spent. We guarantee as long as you include each of the marketing assets on every one of your marketing pieces – you'll see a significant increase in results."

KEY SUMMARY & ACTION POINTS

1. Once you've identified the target market(s), your message should be tailored to focus completely on it.

2. A powerful message is created by using all 9 of the Marketing Assets: (1) UPB, (2) Benefits, (3) Irresistible Offer, (4) Headline, (5) Guarantee, (6) Sales Barrier Demolition, (7) Reasons Why, (8) Social Proof, (9) Call To Action.

3. Time and effort spent on creating well-constructed Marketing Assets will result in a significant improvement in your results.

Agenda Item 6

6. What Marketing Pieces Should We Use To Deliver Our Message?

Introduction

Over the years we've noticed that very few people give any great thought to the types of media they should be using to deliver their message to the target market. More often than not, they simply use the same media that all their competitors are using. This is no different in accountancy.

This could mean two things...

- In most cases the best media isn't being used and, as a result, neither are the best marketing pieces being used to the right target market(s).
- Existing marketing pieces are wasteful.

Furthermore, there can be a huge difference in results if you don't choose the correct media. It's been our experience that many companies leave small fortunes on the table, simply because they have failed to choose the correct media.

The good news is that once you've defined the media (we call this a 'Media Channel') the marketing pieces select themselves (Method – see next agenda item)!

This is a very simple yet highly effective way to determine the right Media Channels to use for your firm.

First let's look at the Media Channels available to you. As you can see, there are just three main Media Channel Categories...

Media Channel Category	Media Channel
1. Published Media	• Classifieds • Newspaper, Magazine & Trade Press • Yellow Pages® • Inserts • Radio • TV • Press Releases • Etc.
2. Direct Marketing Media	• Fax • Seminars • Sales Letters • Lead Generation Letters • Postcards • Flyers • Joint Ventures • Newsletters • Leaflets • Telemarketing • Networking • Etc.
3. E-Media	• Website • Search Engines • Pay Per Click Search Engines • Social Media • eBay • Etc.

So how do you choose the right Media Channel Category and combination of Media Channels for your practice?

All you need to do is ask yourself the following two simple questions...

6. What marketing Pieces Should We Use?

"Where can the target market be reached?"

"Where would the target market look to source our accountancy services?"

The answers to these two questions will help you to determine which Media Channel and marketing pieces to use...

CHOOSING THE RIGHT MEDIA CHANNELS		
Where can the target market be found?	**Media Category**	**Media Channel**
At work (or in the business)	Direct Marketing Media	• Fax • Seminars • Sales Letter • Postcards • Flyers • Joint Ventures • Newsletters • Leaflets • Telemarketing
At home	Direct Marketing Media	• Fax (you wouldn't use fax because very few people have fax machines at home unless the target market was 'people with offices at home') • Seminars • Sales Letter • Postcards • Flyers

		• Joint Ventures • Newsletters • Leaflets • Telemarketing
Yellow Pages	Published Media	• Yellow Pages®
Trade Press	Published Media	• Classifieds • Trade Press • Inserts • Press Releases
Internet	E-Media	• Website • Search Engines • Pay Per Click Search Engines • Social Media
Local newspaper	Published Media	• Classifieds • Newspaper • Inserts • Press Releases

And as you can see from the table above, once you've created your Media Channel list you can then very easily select your marketing pieces for each media.

BLACK & GREY ACCOUNTANTS

Black & Grey don't really understand the true implications of choosing the correct media and the positive effect using multiple media can have on the growth of the firm.

So they decide to use 'direct marketing media' and 'e-media' but don't give any thought to how best they can reach their target market.

AFG Accountants LLP

"You see, once you ask and answer these two questions, you can choose the right media to reach your target market. It really is that simple, but this is one of the most important steps you can take.

"Of course, because people prefer to consume different media and prefer to respond to different media, you never know which is best for each individual, which is why we advocate a multi-media approach. Again tests have shown that mixing media, as opposed to using just one, significantly increases results.

"Therefore you will use all 3 media categories to deliver your message to the target market."

Key Summary & Action Points

1. There are three media categories (1) Published Media, (2) Direct Marketing Media and (3) E-Media.
2. Because people differ in what media they consume, you should use all three media categories to deliver your message to the target market.

AGENDA ITEM 7

7. HOW MANY TIMES SHOULD WE CONTACT THE TARGET MARKET?

INTRODUCTION

There has been much debate about how many times prospects should be contacted. There is no definitive answer, but what we do know is it needs to be more than once – several more. To explain why you need multiple contacts, you need to first understand a little-known but proven phenomenon (we call it the 'Moment') that when used correctly will multiply the number of enquiries and ultimately new clients you get.

It also goes some way to explaining why most accountants think marketing doesn't work. 'Moment' is the fourth of the '5 Ms Of Marketing Your Accountancy Firm'.

So let's start with a simple question...

How many times a year do you currently contact your target market?

If it's any number less than 6 you're turning away thousands and thousands of pounds in new client fees.

It is highly unlikely that you will have sent a marketing piece to any of your potential clients EVERY other month – indeed our research has shown that accountancy firms who do bother to market to their potential clients, on average only send 2 or 3 pieces a year to them.

THIS IS ANOTHER REASON WHY MOST MARKETING DOESN'T WORK.

Tests have proved that repetitive marketing yields far greater returns than ad-hoc marketing. That's why our recommendation is for you to send a marketing piece every 2 months to your potential clients. This will give you the best results.

Why does this work so well?

Repetitive marketing takes advantage of what we call the 'The Moving Parade'. It exists in every market (not just yours), but fewer than 1 in 10,000 businesses are aware of it, or how to use it in order to quickly grow their businesses.

So what is 'The Moving Parade' and how can you use it to your advantage?

Selling any product or service is all about timing. Just because someone isn't interested in buying the product or service today, it doesn't mean they aren't going to be interested tomorrow.

That is in essence what 'The Moving Parade' is all about. Let us explain this further...

Let's say that at the moment you're really happy with your car. You've got no intention of changing it. Therefore every advert, every mailing or any contact you have with a car dealer or car manufacturer is wasted on you.

Letters go in the bin without a second thought. You pick up your newspaper when the adverts come on TV. You simply aren't interested. And nothing will prompt you at this stage to even consider changing your car.

However, three months later your circumstances have changed. You need to do more travelling, and so you decide it's time to look for a more suitable car.

Now every mailing, advert, or communication to do with cars is instantly given attention by you. You're 'in the market' for a new car and you develop an insatiable appetite to find out as much as you can about the cars which would suit you best.

7. How Many Times Should We Make Contact?

This happens all day, every day, as people buy products and services. It is even more intensified with people buying accountancy services.

If you don't keep in touch regularly with your prospects (and clients) you'll never get 'lucky' with the timing as people move in and out of the market, depending on changing circumstances (see diagram on the next page).

By keeping in contact at least once every two months the chance that you will hit the prospect at the right time is increased tenfold.

THE MOVING PARADE – WHAT IT LOOKS LIKE

People/Businesses Who Aren't In A Position To Buy – AT THE MOMENT
These people outside the 'Buying Mode' circle are in your target market or niche but for a number of reasons they will not buy at the moment.

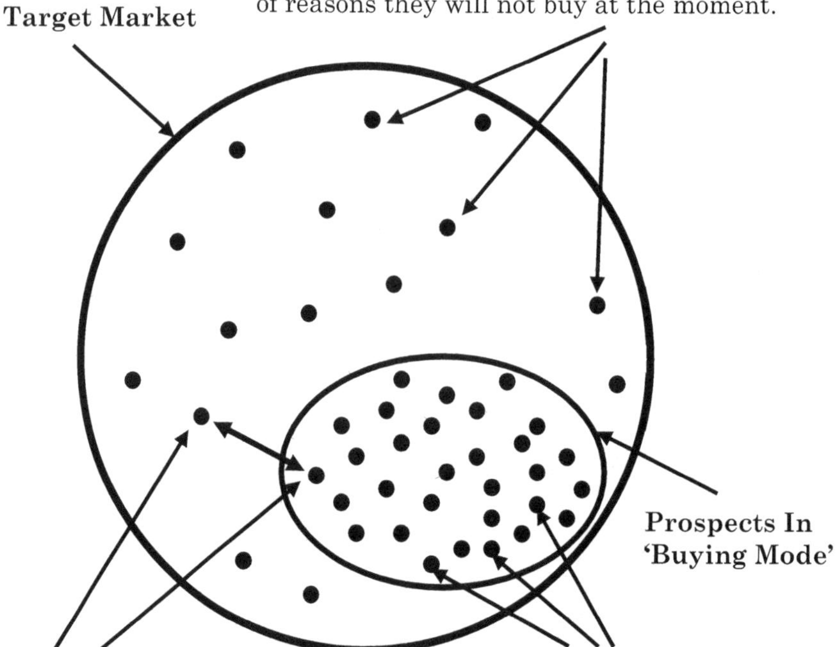

The Moving Parade: People/Businesses That Either Become Buyers Or Non-Buyers
People or businesses move in and out of 'buying mode' all the time. Circumstances change, resulting in people or businesses either becoming buyers or non-buyers. This movement in and out of 'buying mode' is what we call The Moving Parade.

People/Businesses Who Are Ready To Buy Right Now
These people inside the 'Buying Mode' circle are ready to buy right now – remember, they can only buy from YOU or your competitors.

Using a range of stand-out marketing pieces helps you win a large proportion of these clients.

The Result
Using The Moving Parade to your advantage by constantly keeping in touch with the target market, and your clients, means when movement occurs out of non-buying mode into buying mode by any prospect, you have a high probability of getting the sale.

The fear that some accountants have is that they will be seen to be somehow 'unprofessional' by bombarding their target market with junk mail. Well, we have news for you...

Marketing your business effectively is about as professional as you can get. Thoughtful use of our Marketing Assets will only improve the market's perception of your firm, so providing you don't breach ethical guidelines (and nothing we advocate does this) then you can only win – and win BIG!

Taking advantage of The Moving Parade is a very-easy-to-use strategy and one that will provide excellent results for firms who grasp it. So, as we mentioned earlier, our recommendation is for you to send one stand-out marketing piece every two months to your target market. This will automatically result in big increases in enquiries for your accountancy practice.

BLACK & GREY ACCOUNTANTS

Unfortunately Black & Grey have no idea about The Moving Parade and like most other firms hope that one or at the most two approaches to their target market will suffice. They may get lucky but the level of response they receive will be low – very low.

AFG ACCOUNTANTS LLP

"This is one of the most important things you can learn when growing your accountancy firm. The Moving Parade is such an important phenomenon that you have to use it to your advantage.

"The only way to do that is to set up a frequency of contact that takes away the 'luck' factor and instead enables you to have a contact strategy that maximises the chances of you 'catching' someone, just when they're thinking of changing their accountants.

"Remember, you have no way of knowing when a prospect's circumstances are about to change. It could be an unexpected bill or a missed deadline. It could be an unsatisfactory resolution to a problem or just a mistake. Or just a culmination of a small number of things that cause frustration. But no matter what the circumstance, you have to give yourself the best chance of getting the call. The only way to do that is to get your firm's name in front of them at regular intervals throughout the year. That's the only way we know how to get 'lucky'. But boy does it work!

"With one marketing piece you may only get 0.5% or less as a response. But with 6 or more well-constructed marketing pieces, strategically sent to the prospect throughout the year, responses will often multiply.

"We recommend a minimum of 6 contacts sent to your target market in January, March, May, July, September and November."

KEY SUMMARY & ACTION POINTS

1. The Moving Parade is an important phenomenon that explains how a change in circumstances leads to people moving in and out of 'buying mode'.

2. You can take advantage of The Moving Parade by contacting your target market several times a year (ideally 6 or more times per year).

AGENDA ITEM 8

8. HOW DO WE CREATE MARKETING PIECES THAT GET RESULTS?

INTRODUCTION

We have now reached the last of the '5 Ms Of Marketing Your Accountancy Firm'.

This last 'M' is another big reason why so many marketing campaigns fail – the method used in the media to deliver the message just doesn't work.

In other words, you could have got all previous 'M's in place - right market, right message, right media and right moment - but the actual device itself just doesn't work.

For example, all 4 'M's are in place, yet let's say the advert used in the magazine wasn't put together using all the Marketing Assets, and those that were included weren't used correctly. You see, not only do all the Marketing Assets need to be used in each marketing piece – there is also a RIGHT and WRONG way to create the piece itself.

This final piece of the jigsaw is so, so important. It also includes how you get your marketing piece noticed. For example, numerous tests have shown that using handwritten names and addresses and multiple stamps on the front of an envelope works more than 9 times better (that's NOT a mistake!) than a label and a franking machine.

So to get results from your marketing pieces they have to be created, based on the following three elements (otherwise they will fail – or at least won't work as well as you'd hoped)...

- Marketing Assets – all the marketing assets must be included as your message.

- The Right Format – we spoke earlier about the right and wrong ways of creating each marketing piece.

- Stand-Out Appeal – if your marketing piece doesn't rise above the clutter and get noticed it will die a horrible death (most marketing pieces never pass this test).

BLACK & GREY ACCOUNTANTS

Like most people and most firms, Black & Grey take the view that they will be able to create their own marketing pieces. There's nothing wrong with this at all, but if you do go down the 'do it yourself' route you must invest some time and money in relevant books, seminars and courses to see how to do it.

For the cost of just £20 or £30 you can buy a book written by an expert that shows you how to create ads, sales letters, seminars, websites, you name it – and as long as you research wisely, for less than a good meal for two you can give yourself a much better chance of success.

Yet most people won't even do this. Sure there are many books full of worthless theories on how to do it, but books like this one, where the author(s) has genuinely been there, done it and got the T-shirt and will give you the tricks of the trade, DO exist!

But Black & Grey do what most people do and decide to create their marketing pieces 'in-house'. After all, they think, it can't be that hard to get results. But without seeking out expertise even in the form of a book, their chances of success are low – very low.

AFG ACCOUNTANTS LLP

"As we mentioned above, it's the combination of these three elements which helps to transform any marketing piece into a winner. And often it takes trial and error to achieve success. We've explained about the 9 Marketing Assets and what you need to do to create them.

“Next, the right format is crucial for your marketing pieces to be successful. For example, almost every accountant’s website fails in terms of generating enquiries. In all our years not one accountant has come to us and said, ‘I have a great website that keeps churning out enquiries’. That’s because the format is wrong. All wrong.

“You see, aesthetically and functionality wise, most websites are fine. The problem occurs because they are created not to generate enquiries but to look impressive and show a professional image of the firm. Sure a site like this adds credibility (an important element) but without a focus on generating enquiries, it fails to deliver.

“So what do you do to make it work? This is the ‘how’ and it’s not that difficult. All you need is a stand-alone web page that focuses on your target market and then delivers the message to them using the Marketing Assets. The single goal of that page is to generate the enquiry, which is usually a request for a meeting. Tests have repeatedly shown that there should be no outgoing links to any other page or website. Complete focus on the objective is what brings results.

“But to really make your marketing pieces work they have to stand out. This is the third and final piece of the success jigsaw. You see, not only does your firm have to differentiate itself from the competition to attract and retain clients – the same can be said about your marketing.

“People are subjected to hundreds of marketing messages every day. You have to rise above this ‘clutter’ to get noticed.

“If your marketing is like everyone else’s it just won’t get noticed. And remember, you’re not just competing with other firms of accountants for your target market’s attention – you’re competing with every other type of business which is marketing to them.

"In reality that's a daunting prospect and explains why most marketing doesn't work – none of it rises above the clutter and 95% of it goes straight in the bin or simply isn't even noticed.

"So now you know why most marketing fails or never reaches the level it should. The message is wrong, the format is wrong and it never rises above the clutter. In many respects this last piece of the puzzle is the most important. You see, you can have the best message and format, but if no one notices it – it will still fail.

"That's why we advise you to look at what other people are doing with their marketing. Pay close attention to the types of media you've chosen to use to reach your target market. For example, if you're going to use lead generation letters, what formats do you receive through your own mail at home and at work that stand out for you? What gimmicks stand out? What letters ethically force you to respond? The chances are you can mimic and swipe these approaches and tailor them to your own firm.

"But above all else don't be boring. The further away from this stereotype most people have about accountants, the more successful you'll become. You see, with marketing pieces that rise above the clutter, you put your firm on a different level to all other accountancy firms. You cannot underestimate the effect being different with your marketing can have on your firm.

"For instance, let's use the lead generation letter as an example. Most accountants will of course do their level best to write a professional letter. It won't include the right message but it's okay, and the format they choose is a basic two-page letter. Again that's fine. The problem is they send it in a plain white envelope, with the contact details printed on to a label (it's easier to do this – they think) and franked.

"They send this out and wonder why they didn't get a response. And it's simple. They could have been giving away £50 notes inside the envelope, but 99% of people didn't even open it. Why? Because it smacks of 'junk mail' and it looks like 95% of other marketing that arrives on their desk.

"You see, whether you like it or not, we all subconsciously have two piles in our mind when we're sorting mail. We have Pile A and Pile B. Pile A is stuff that looks uninteresting and like junk. It takes us approximately half a second to decide this. Yes, just half a second. Pile B, on the other hand, is stuff that looks interesting. Stuff that we will either open right now, or leave to open later. If your letter isn't on Pile B you've had it. That's why it needs to rise above the clutter and look interesting. Most letters unfortunately go on Pile A. They are doomed to failure just because of this.

"But now you know this, you can do something about it. The rule is simple. Never, ever, use a marketing piece that looks boring. Never, ever, use a marketing piece that looks like junk. Never, ever, use a marketing piece that doesn't rise above the clutter. Do this and we promise your results will astonish you."

KEY SUMMARY & ACTION POINTS

1. Getting results from your marketing pieces is difficult unless you ensure they have a complete message, use the right format and have stand-out appeal.

2. Never spend money on a marketing piece unless it adheres to (1) above, otherwise you might as well throw money down the toilet – you wouldn't do that, so don't do it with your marketing pieces.

Agenda Item 9

9. How Do We Get More Referrals?

Introduction

You should now have a good understanding of the 5 Ms Of Marketing Your Accountancy Firm. To recap, here they are...

- Market: Who you are targeting (your 'Target Market').
- Message: Why someone should use your firm rather than anyone else (your competitors) and what you need to convey in your message to get people to respond and buy.
- Media: The marketing channels you will use to deliver your message to the market (i.e. website, adverts, direct mail, articles, etc.).
- Moment: Timing is everything!
- Method: What 'marketing piece' will you use for each media to rise above the clutter and get noticed over EVERY other business that's marketing to your target market (notice this is other accountants AND every other type of business trying to get your potential clients to buy from them).

These five core elements need to be the focus of your growth across the 4 Practice Multipliers. Again to recap, here they are...

- Referral
- General Marketing
- Sales Conversion
- Maximising Fee Income

So let's start with referral.

Our research has shown that accountants acquire 93% of their new clients by referral. That's a huge number which highlights two key issues...

1. In general, accountants are very good at converting referral enquiries into clients.
2. Unfortunately it also demonstrates a lack of application in non-referral techniques (General Marketing).

We also learnt that 97% of accountants are dissatisfied with the volume of referrals they actually generate, whether through clients or other referral sources such as the banks, solicitors, IFAs and others. In other words, they believe they should do a whole lot better.

There are three significant reasons for this 'underachievement'...

- REASON #1: APATHY

  Most people simply don't recommend their accountant because they have no cause to. The referral process for accountants is a reactive one (people only ever suggest an accountant if they are asked. This is because they have no real reason to enthuse about their accountants). Yes all good businesses get referrals, but clients need to have a reason and/or an incentive to recommend other people. We call the incentive a 'Customer Incentive Reward Scheme'.

9. How Do We Get More Referrals?

Putting in place a Customer Incentive Reward Scheme (alongside a Unique Perceived Benefit – we covered this when we discussed the message) which focuses on getting referrals is one of the easiest and most beneficial things you can do.

A structured Customer Incentive Reward Scheme when combined with your Unique Perceived Benefit will give your firm the following benefits:

- A constant supply of quality referrals.
- Increased enthusiasm dealing with people who are highly interested in your services.
- An increase in the quality of clients.
- Increased profits. You spend less time and money converting referred people. They have already been recommended and therefore trust is already established.
- As a result, referred people tend to value your services more than an 'ordinary' prospect. They usually don't 'shop around' to get the best price. This means you'll be able to sell your services at an optimum price (or at least at a good level).
- An effective Customer Incentive Reward Scheme will help strengthen relationships with your clients. By helping their friends, colleagues and business associates, you make clients look good in the eyes of their peers.

IMPORTANT NOTE:

If you've tried a Customer Incentive Reward Scheme before without success (like many other firms) there are two simple reasons why it probably didn't work as well as you had hoped: (1) see reason #2 below, and (2) because the marketing pieces you used to promote the scheme weren't effective (see 'Method' above).

So please don't say to yourself – "We've tried this before and it didn't work – so I'm not trying it again". The simple fact is they DO work; you just have to know how to do it.

- REASON #2: NO DISCERNIBLE DIFFERENCE BETWEEN ACCOUNTANTS

  Just being a good accountant isn't sufficient. You see, as you know, most people think all accountants are the same. Why would they recommend their accountant to someone else when they think all accountants are identical?

- REASON #3: NO SYSTEM

  Research has shown that some two-thirds of clients say they are prepared to recommend their accountants to others, but only 6% say they have ever been asked.

  That's a shocking statistic, but shows that most accountants just don't have any system in place for requesting referrals from clients. If you don't ask – you don't get.

The good news is there is a simple formula you can use to rapidly improve the number of referrals you get...

The Formula For Getting A Constant Stream Of Referrals

(1) Good Accountant

+

(2) Referral System (Customer Incentive Reward Scheme)

+

(3) Highly Sought-After Uniqueness

+

(4) Effective Communication Of Scheme

=

Constant Stream Of Referrals

You need **ALL 4** elements of the formula to really motivate people to recommend you. If you're missing just one of these elements, then the number of referrals you get is significantly reduced.

Now, we're taking it for granted that you offer a good level of service to your clients, therefore you need to focus on creating a 'highly sought-after uniqueness' (you should already have some thoughts about this as we discussed it earlier), together with a 'Customer Incentive Reward Scheme'.

A Customer Incentive Reward Scheme is literally the system you use to ensure ALL clients are aware that you want referrals, and the incentive can be anything from vouchers, money off their services, or anything you believe will incentivise your clients to give you more referrals. Experience has shown us that the more generous you are – the more you get.

One thing to think about with referrals and the incentives you offer clients is that a referral doesn't cost you anything to get.

Therefore, other than the cost of your incentive, your acquisition cost is ZERO. So you can 'afford' to spend more on the incentive to acquire the referral in the first place.

As we explained earlier, the 'highly sought-after uniqueness' is a more challenging element for you to create. You have to come up with something that's not only highly desired by your clients and potential clients, but something that your competitors don't offer. But hopefully you have some ideas on this already.

And finally you need an effective method to communicate the referral scheme to your clients (and third-party referral sources such as solicitors and IFAs).

What you need here is something that really stands out and ensures clients, and other third-party referral sources, are motivated and excited about the scheme once they read or listen to your message.

It really is that simple. But as we explained, all three components are essential if you are looking to ramp up your referrals.

BLACK & GREY ACCOUNTANTS

At least Black & Grey are seriously thinking about how they can get more referrals. Like most firms they find themselves frustrated in the knowledge that they offer a good service to most, if not all clients, and it puzzles them why they don't get more.

They decide that the best way to get more referrals is to ask clients at the end of each client meeting. That's better than nothing, and to a certain extent should generate a few more referrals.

But, because they don't have all the component parts of a successful referral system, they will still feel frustrated at the lack of success they achieve in this area and, even though they know they should be doing it, some people in the firm still shy away from asking the question. But nevertheless, it's a step in the right direction.

AFG ACCOUNTANTS LLP

"You see, you can't blame your clients for not giving you more referrals. If you don't have a system in place, you're leaving the growth of your firm in this area down to fate. You have no control over the process and without a system you will never ever generate the level of referrals you feel you deserve.

"Once you've decided on your uniqueness, you can then agree what incentive you're going to use. Giving clients a percentage off their next annual bill almost always works well, as does giving them free (not discounted) services.

"You just need to decide on what you believe will be the most attractive incentive to give your clients and then start promoting it to them, first by letter, and then by making sure at client meetings it is an agenda item to discuss.

"This is your SYSTEM. Yes it's that simple. The key, like for everything we're telling you today, is to follow through. Putting the referral system on your agendas ensures partners, managers and other client-facing staff don't forget to keep asking for referrals – it's easy to forget (or avoid) if it's not written down!"

KEY SUMMARY & ACTION POINTS

1. You can increase your referrals as long as you put a system in place.
2. Key to a successful referral system is to combine your uniqueness with a good incentive, and to then communicate it at every opportunity to clients and third-party referral sources.
3. You will need different incentives for third-party referral sources and clients.

AGENDA ITEM 10

10. HOW DO WE GET MORE CLIENTS FROM GENERAL MARKETING ACTIVITIES?

INTRODUCTION

"But Marketing Doesn't Work"

In the last section we pointed out that only 7% of new clients come from non-referral sources (general marketing activities), which means there is much more business to be gained by proactively targeting the right businesses, using proven non-referral techniques.

If you could generate the same amount (or more) of clients using general marketing techniques as you do with referral techniques – this would have a huge impact on your practice.

So why is it that accountants shy away from using general marketing methods? We've discovered a few reasons...

1. Most accountants have tried a number of non-referral techniques but, because they got poor results, they conclude they don't work.

2. In most cases it's not that the strategy doesn't work – it's because the techniques used were poor – resulting in less than acceptable results (we see this a lot in most other industries too).

3. Other methods such as telemarketing, seminars and articles (which are used with varying degrees of success by many firms) would be significantly more successful with the right methodology.

IMPORTANT NOTE:

Reasons '2' and '3' above are caused by people NOT using the '5 Ms Of Marketing Your Accountancy Firm'.

But with the right execution and using the right approach you can get excellent results from all the following general marketing activities...

- Direct mail (letters, postcards, etc.) – Still by far THE best method for generating enquiries for accountants!
- Press Releases
- Special Reports/Articles
- Newspaper / Magazine Ads
- Classified Ads
- Yellow Pages Ads (yes, with the right ad, Yellow Pages advertising is still very successful for accountancy firms)
- Networking (with innovative thought-provoking scripts / presentations)
- Business Cards (not like conventional business cards)
- Websites
- Google AdWords
- Social Media (Facebook, etc.)

There are of course other marketing activities you can use, but the ones listed above will give you the best return for the least time, effort and cost. Believe us, we've tested these and many others to find the most potent strategies for growing accountancy firms.

IMPORTANT NOTE ABOUT YOUR CHOICE OF GENERAL MARKETING ACTIVITIES

Our advice with every marketing activity you consider is to only use those that give you a return for the minimal time and effort. Even if something is 'FREE' (i.e. Facebook) there is still a cost – based on the time you put in. Time, or more accurately a lack of time, is the one thing that will restrict you in the growth of your firm. So the more economical you are with your use of it and the more effective you become managing your time – the better.

You should therefore be choosing marketing activities which are kind to you in terms of the time you need to allocate to them and of course the return you get for your efforts.

Only you can decide what's right. But always be mindful of the trade-off you have to make.

The key, as we mentioned above, is to ensure you apply ALL '5 Ms of Marketing For Accountants' to your general marketing activities. This is what gives you leverage. It's these 5 elements that add power to your 'marketing pieces' (the actual marketing piece that you use in each media – i.e. your actual advert, your website, your letter, etc.).

The 5 Ms are in essence what makes marketing work. Without them results are unsatisfactory, but with them – your success is virtually guaranteed!

Black & Grey Accountants

Black & Grey know they need to improve in this area. They know they need to be more active. They, however, face the challenge most firms face, in that they've never really had any success in this area, so they're starting from a blank piece of paper. They don't have a grasp of the 5 Ms so this immediately puts them at a disadvantage, but they're going to choose several activities and see how it goes.

AFG ACCOUNTANTS LLP

"Hopefully you can see how everything is now starting to come together. Applying the 5 Ms to your general marketing activities will ensure your results exceed your expectations, but like everything we advise you to do, you should test before investing large sums in any activity.

"Remember, the big disadvantage you have when you've never used a marketing activity before – is you simply don't know how well it is going to work. Even when you're as experienced as we are, you still need to move forward with caution. We have seen many different businesses, including accountancy firms, lose thousands of pounds, even tens of thousands of pounds, by deciding to go with a certain activity and pumping significant funds into it – only to realise it just doesn't work. It's too late by then. So our advice is to always test small. You can always increase your investment once you know what results your activities are generating.

"For example, let's say you're going to send a lead generation letter to your target market. There are 1,000 businesses in your target market. Let's say, because you've heeded our advice, your letter stands out and as a result your cost including postage works out at, say, £3.00 per letter. The less experienced person would then eagerly mail all 1,000 businesses at a cost of £3,000. The more experienced would mail, say, 200 each of two different versions, at a cost of £1,200, and wait to analyse the results before moving forward and mailing the rest.

"Testing two different versions (having changed just one variable such as the headline) will bring you two different results. Let's say letter 1 generated 1 reply and letter 2 generated 3 replies. In other words, letter 2 generated 300% more enquiries (not uncommon when you test). Now we can mail the last 600 with letter 2 which will yield a further 9 replies, totalling 13 responses – not bad. However, if we'd just mailed letter 1 to the 1000 businesses, we'd have only received 5 responses – yet our total costs would be the same.

"Testing is therefore another way to leverage your marketing and the corresponding results. It's how smart marketers always roll out their marketing, especially when they're trying something new.

"Probably the biggest area where accountants, and most other businesses, make this mistake is with their website. Several thousand pounds are often spent creating a site with bells and whistles on. It looks great but doesn't generate any tangible results.

"So we advise you to be pragmatic with all your marketing spend, until you have concrete results. Yes this process takes longer, but it's by far the most sensible way to grow your firm and, in the long run, will not only help you save thousands of pounds, it will help you generate significantly better results as long as you test.

"In terms of the marketing activities you should use, we've detailed these earlier, but by far the best method is to use direct mail. Even though most firms conclude direct mail doesn't work, when you apply the 5 Ms your results will surprise you and occasionally will astonish you."

KEY SUMMARY & ACTION POINTS

1. You are seriously hindering your growth if you don't use general marketing activities.
2. As long as you apply the 5 Ms to your general marketing activities, there's no reason why you can't achieve at least moderate success.
3. For activities which you've never used before, make sure you test small and only invest more heavily once you know it works.
4. When testing, only change one variable at a time. If you change more than one, you'll never know which variable worked.

Agenda Item 11

11. How Do We Convert More Enquiries Into Good Clients?

Introduction

As we've discovered, many business owners (including accountants) spend a considerable amount of time, energy and money in order to generate enquiries.

However, there's little point generating dozens of enquiries each month from referral and general marketing activities if you only convert a small percentage of them – it's a huge missed opportunity!

The process of converting enquiries into clients is called 'Sales Conversion' and is the third Practice Multiplier.

Our experience has shown that accountants in general are poor at converting enquiries into clients, particularly from non-referral enquiries.

You're probably saying to yourself, "I convert most of my referrals anyway, so what's the point in putting in a system for converting them?" Well the point is this – no one converts at 100%, so the closer you can get to this target the more clients you'll acquire.

If one of your objectives is to target either better clients or a new market location, then your conversion system becomes even more relevant. Your existing referrals come from existing contacts in your existing market. They are already warm leads, half convinced before they even walk through your door, because they have already been told that you are the accountant for them.

Your conversion rate should be very high in these circumstances but your performance at these meetings is largely irrelevant when it comes to meeting cold leads.

Furthermore, when it comes to general marketing, you are much more likely to be in a competitive situation (even if it's only with the incumbent accountant) – so your conversion of these types of enquiry will undoubtedly be lower – probably much lower. Plus, what we are talking about here, and throughout this book, is acquiring the right type of clients at the right fees.

Be honest...

How often do you sneak a peek at last year's bill from the incumbent firm before talking about your fees? Anyone can convert at a low price... it's how well you do at higher prices that counts. So a sales conversion system will improve results considerably – even if and when you start increasing your fees.

As soon as an enquiry is created (either from your referral or general marketing activities), you need to have a 'SYSTEM' (yes, a system!) in order to convert as many as you can into good-quality clients.

Concentrating more on converting enquiries into clients will ensure two things:

1. You'll rapidly transform the practice

2. You'll maximise the return on investment the firm makes on ALL its referral and general marketing strategies

The good news is that putting in place a system to convert more enquiries into clients costs very little (if anything at all) and the results are instant!

So What Is a Sales Conversion System?

In simple terms a sales conversion system is a system used to ensure the practice generates more clients from the number of enquiries generated.

It starts the moment the enquiry is received, and continues right through to the point when that enquiry becomes a client.

One of the HUGE hidden benefits of a successful system is that the process of converting enquiries is driven by the system, rather than the individual – which means anyone (with the right experience in the firm) can use the system to great effect (which also helps with *succession*).

Let's not understate this point. You convert potential clients at a meeting through your experience of handling many such meetings, and through your experience of dealing with hundreds of clients.

You have a wealth of case history and confidence that you can apply. More junior members of your firm don't have this. The only way to replace it is to give them a system that they can apply which actually works. This removes the randomness of an approach, that to be honest relies on clients taking the decision that they like you.

Your current resources are expanded significantly if others can win clients. Furthermore, your succession options increase as your staff develop, not only because their client performance and inter-relationships improve, but because you are more able to take a back seat.

Here's a simple diagram explaining why you need a sales conversion system...

The Effect Of Positive Contacts In The Sales Cycle

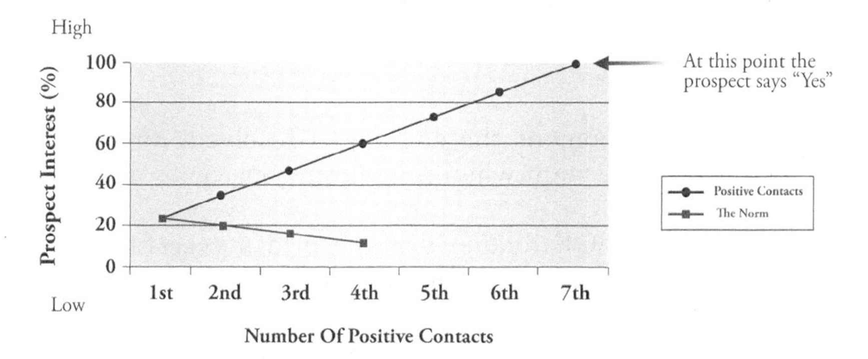

The Norm – By the fourth contact the prospect's interest is lower than where it started. They are now further away from the sale! That's why 90% of sales people have given up!

Positive Contacts – By the fourth contact the prospect's interest is high. Now it's only a matter of time and a couple more positive contacts before the sale is made.

What this chart shows is that the prospect must reach a certain level of interest before he or she is prepared to say "Yes" and buy your accountancy services.

Therefore, what you need to do is increase the prospect's interest each time the firm makes contact with them. A contact can be a meeting, a letter, a fax, an e-mail – or any way in which you make contact with prospects.

Research has shown that on average it takes 7 positive contacts ('The Rule of 7') before the prospect says, "Yes".

A sales conversion system should therefore automatically cater for these contacts, which in turn will increase the chances of getting a positive result with the vast majority of prospects.

Your sales conversion system should focus on each stage and as a result many more enquiries will turn into clients.

11. How Do We Convert More Enquiries?

...and there's one more important piece of the jigsaw to consider. We call it the 'Follow-Up Ladder'.

You see, Follow-Up is not practised by many businesses (particularly accountancy firms – think about it, how many positive contacts do you have at the moment from the enquiry to the sale?). This means those that follow up correctly will always gain more clients.

To reinforce this point further, we think you'll find these research results very interesting...

- A recent study conducted by Performark (a research company in the USA) showed how few companies follow up properly or even at all.

  They found that out of 10,000 advertising enquiries – 22% never received the information they requested, 45% received the information more than 65 days after their request, for 12% it took more than 120 days to receive their information, and 87% were never contacted by a sales representative.

- A recent study by Thomas Publishing Company showed that most salespeople give up too early, regardless of the industry.

  According to the study, 80% of sales to business are made on the fifth sales call, but only 10% of salespeople call more than three times (the diagram on page 104 shows the complete details of the study).

- A recent study conducted by Tom Rayfield, a UK direct marketing expert, showed that companies are very poor at follow-up. Taking 200 randomly selected advertisers, he replied to them all to measure follow-up responses.

  To his amazement, the average time taken for people to reply to him was eight days, and 17 companies (8.5%) didn't even bother to reply!

- Dr Geoffrey Lant, the renowned marketing and research consultant, reasons that most buying decisions are made after seven contacts over an 18-month period. He calls this the 'Rule of 7', and many more studies support this.

What you need to do is make a positive impression on the prospect at each contact. By doing this, you speed up the sales cycle and keep more prospects in it – resulting in more sales.

If one of your contacts has a less than positive impact on your prospect, their interest drops, making it harder for you to close the sale. This is a basic but very important tactic for you to apply and understand. The diagram on the next page shows how it all fits together...

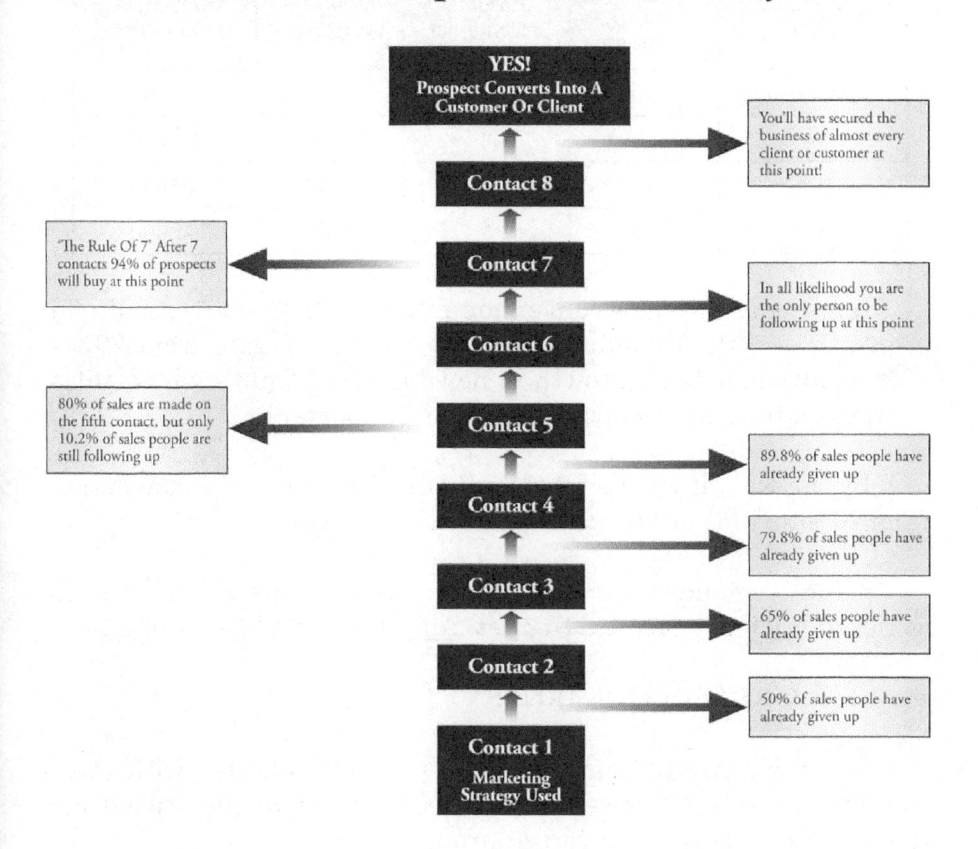

WHY A SALES CONVERSION SYSTEM IS SO POWERFUL, AND WHY YOUR FIRM MUST HAVE ONE

Let's just take this hypothetical situation...

Let's say, at the moment, your practice converts 20% of general marketing enquiries into clients. The average fee income is £1,000, and 10 enquiries are generated each month. Look at the table below and see the effect a sales conversion system can have on the business in just 12 months:

CONVERSION RATE	ENQUIRIES PER MONTH	CUSTOMERS PER MONTH	AVERAGE ORDER (£)	ANNUAL FEE INCOME (£)
20%	10	2	1000	24,000
30%	10	3	1000	36,000
40%	10	4	1000	48,000
50%	10	5	1000	60,000

Improving the sales conversion rate from 20% - 30% results in a growth of 50%. Doubling the sales conversion rate from 20% - 40% results in a 100% growth in new business. That's why a sales conversion process is so powerful and so important.

By the way, if you think it's difficult to improve the conversion from 20% to 40%, or 30% to 60%, or more – it isn't!

...and remember, improving the sales conversion rate is achieved **without any extra cost**. And that's the beauty of it!

BLACK & GREY ACCOUNTANTS

Black & Grey recognise that they could do better with their enquiry conversion. However, they feel content in the knowledge that for referrals they convert at around 75%.

What they fail to recognise is their conversion of general marketing enquiries is lower – much lower, and if they decide to increase their fees (which is on the agenda) their conversion of referral enquiries will also plummet.

Like most businesses and accountancy firms, Black & Grey give little thought to how they can improve their conversion rate, so it will be interesting to see how they do in the coming months!

AFG ACCOUNTANTS LLP

"So putting in a sales conversion system gives you real leverage. You don't need any fancy software or any complicated system. You just need to plan each contact so the prospect gets wowed each time.

"For example, one of the points of contact that is almost always very weak is parking for the prospect when they arrive for the meeting at the accountant's offices. Even if you have no on-site parking there are many things that can be done to make this part of the system a real positive experience for the prospect.

"You're lucky you do have on-site parking, but we noticed as we arrived that it was full. We parked at a pay-and-display 5 minutes walk away. We're pretty sure that's also the experience prospects have when they come to meet you. So now we've brought this to your attention, what can you do to make parking a real wow moment for the prospect?

"You see, because so few firms really look at the detail of these points of contact, it's easy to score big points against them, especially when you're in competition with them. The likelihood that they have also thought carefully about these contact points is remote – so you win and you win big.

"It's these points of contact and how well you administer them that set apart the good from the great. More importantly, when you look to increase your fees, this makes a big difference to your conversion. So a sales conversion system will give you the ability to convert more enquiries (referral and general marketing) into clients and at the right fee level, all with zero cost.

"Plus, there is a number of what we call 'sales conversion strategies' that really help to convert the prospect. For example, Marketing Assets such as guarantees, sales barrier demolition, and social proof are excellent 'sales converters' that again cost nothing to apply.

"That's the sort of leverage any business would love – and you can get it instantly."

KEY SUMMARY & ACTION POINTS

1. A sales conversion system is a series of positive contact points and sales conversion strategies you put in place to increase the interest and desire of the prospect, taking them closer and closer to the sale.

2. An effective sales conversion system costs virtually nothing to put in place and the effects are gained instantly.

AGENDA ITEM 12

12. HOW DO WE INCREASE & MAXIMISE FEES?

INTRODUCTION

We can go into almost any accountancy firm and release thousands of pounds of revenue and profit, literally overnight. We can do this NOT because we're expert marketers, but because we tap into 'The Acres Of Diamonds Principle' that every business possesses.

So what is this 'Acres Of Diamonds Principle'? Let us explain...

One of the most interesting Americans who lived in the 19th century was a man by the name of Russell Herman Conwell. He was born in 1843 and lived until 1925. He was a lawyer for about fifteen years until he became a clergyman.

One day, a young man went to him and told him he wanted a college education but couldn't swing it financially. Dr. Conwell decided, at that moment, what his aim in life was – besides being a man of the cloth, that is. He decided to build a university for unfortunate, but deserving, students. He did have a challenge, however. He would need a few million dollars to build the university. For Dr. Conwell, and anyone with real purpose in life, nothing could stand in the way of his goal.

Several years before this incident, Dr. Conwell was tremendously intrigued by a true story – with its ageless moral. The story was about a farmer who lived in Africa and through a visitor became tremendously excited about looking for diamonds.

Diamonds were already discovered in abundance on the African continent and this farmer got so excited about the idea of millions of dollars worth of diamonds that he sold his farm to head out to the diamond line.

He wandered all over the continent, as the years slipped by, constantly searching for diamonds and wealth, which he never found. Eventually he went completely broke and threw himself into a river and drowned.

Meanwhile, the new owner of his farm picked up an unusual-looking rock about the size of a country egg and put it on his mantle as a sort of curiosity.

A visitor stopped by, and viewing the rock, practically went into terminal convulsions.

He told the new owner of the farm that the funny-looking rock on his mantle was about the biggest diamond that had ever been found. The new owner of the farm said, "Heck, the whole farm is covered with them" – and sure enough it was.

The farm turned out to be the Kimberley Diamond Mine...the richest the world has ever known. The original farmer was literally standing on 'Acres of Diamonds' until he sold his farm.

Dr. Conwell learned from the story of the farmer and continued to teach its moral. Each of us is right in the middle of our own 'Acre of Diamonds', if only we would realise it and develop the ground we are standing on before charging off in search of greener pastures.

Dr. Conwell told this story many times and attracted enormous audiences. He told the story long enough to raise the money to start the college for underprivileged deserving students. In fact, he raised nearly six million dollars and the university he founded, Temple University in Philadelphia, has at least ten degree-granting colleges and six other schools.

12. How Do We Increase & Maximise Fees?

When Dr Russell H. Conwell talked about each of us being right on our own 'Acre of Diamonds', he meant it. This story does not get old...it will be true forever... Opportunity does not just come along – it is there all the time – we just have to see it.

So how does this relate to you and your accountancy firm?

Well, by far and away the most lucrative part of your business is your clients...

It's the clients who are your own 'Acres Of Diamonds'.

Once a new client is acquired it's your 'duty' to provide them with more value, more service and more benefits.

This is known as 'Back-End Selling'.

Therefore you need to put in place a system for increasing the monetary value of each client to you. There are just 3 key areas to focus on...

1. Client Retention
2. Increasing Fees
3. Selling More Services

Let's take a look at each one...

1. Client Retention

Although many accountants believe they don't have a problem with retention, it's fair to say that if they could still retain a few of those who DO leave each year, it will amount to a significant sum over time.

A more accurate view for many firms would be to say that they don't have a retention problem today.

For a start, all clients will eventually retire, sell, die or go bust. Secondly, most clients don't move simply because they don't perceive that they have better options. In other words, firms keep clients because the competition hasn't got their marketing act together. This is changing!

The good news is there are some very simple strategies to follow, which have a major impact on your retention of clients....

Proven strategies that help improve retention are...

- Unique Competitive Advantage (we've already covered this earlier)
- Moments Of Truth (see below)
- Managing Your Client Base (see below)

MOMENTS OF TRUTH

So let's first look at Moments Of Truth and how you can use it to transform how you work with your clients...

Moments Of Truth goes to the heart of growing your accountancy firm in this new economy. We're going to explain how you can transform the experience every client has with you – so they not only stay with you for longer, but they also refer you more frequently and are much less resistant to fee increases.

This added value approach may sound hard to believe, but in the next few minutes you'll see for yourself just how powerful Moments Of Truth can be.

So what exactly is Moments Of Truth? Let us explain...

In 1987 Jan Carlzon, the CEO of Scandinavian Airlines, wrote the book, 'Moments Of Truth'. It explained how he took the airline from deficit to profit by 'moving' the airline to a customer-focused organisation.

Now, as you know, there have been many books written on customer service, but where this book and Carlzon's strategies really differ, is his focus on each interaction the customer has with the business. He calls these 'Moments of Truth' and, of course, each interaction can be a positive or a negative experience.

Scandinavian Airlines prospered because they worked very hard to make sure each Moment Of Truth with their customers was a very positive experience and the results they achieved were a testament to this.

Take a look at the diagram on the next page. It shows how at each contact (Moment Of Truth) you need to ensure each interaction is a favourable one for your clients.

MOMENTS OF TRUTH EXPLAINED...

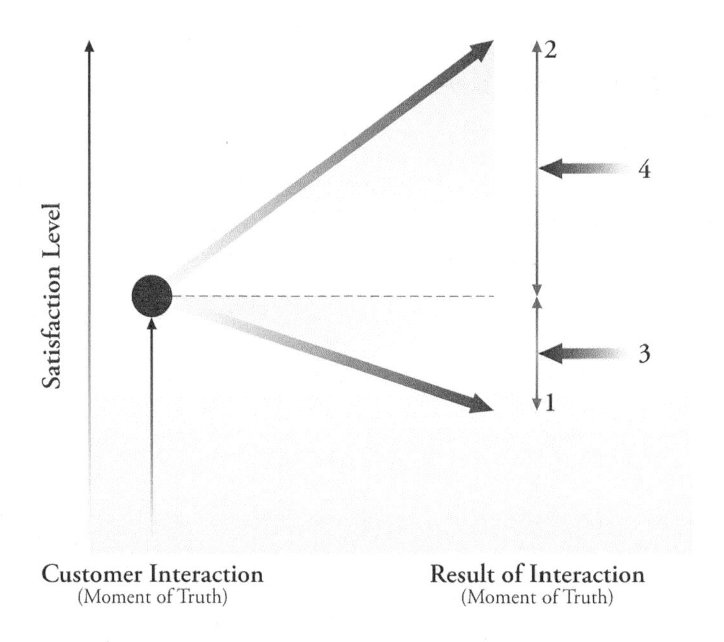

Legend:

1. The effect on the client using traditional marketing strategies. Notice the Moment Of Truth was a negative experience reducing the client's satisfaction – and therefore creating discontent with an existing client.

2. Moments Of Truth Approach. By breaking down each step **even further** the interest level and satisfaction level is raised even higher.

3. Shows the drop in interest level and satisfaction using traditional techniques (or none at all).

4. Shows the increase gained by using Moments Of Truth techniques.

Therefore what you need to do is increase the satisfaction level of each client when any contact occurs (Moment Of Truth).

A contact can be a meeting, a letter, a fax, an e-mail – or any way in which your practice comes into contact with a client.

To explain this point further, and just in case you have any doubts about the power of Moments Of Truth and the effect it can have on your practice, here's a great example of how any industry can capitalise on this fabulous strategy...

Harvey Mackay (author of 'Swim With The Sharks Without Being Eaten Alive') tells a wonderful story about a cab driver that demonstrates Moments Of Truth perfectly...

He was waiting in line for a ride at the airport.

When a cab pulled up, the first thing Harvey noticed was that the taxi was polished to a bright shine.

Smartly dressed in a white shirt, black tie and freshly pressed black trousers, the cab driver jumped out and rounded the car to open the back passenger door for Harvey.

He handed Harvey a laminated card and said:

"I'm Wally, your driver. While I'm loading your bags in the trunk I'd like you to read my mission statement."

Taken aback, Harvey read the card. It said: Wally's Mission Statement:

To get my customers to their destination in the quickest, safest and cheapest way possible in a friendly environment.

This blew Harvey away. Especially when he noticed that the inside of the cab matched the outside. Spotlessly clean!

As he slid behind the wheel, Wally said, "Would you like a cup of coffee? I have a thermos of regular and one of decaf."

Harvey said jokingly, "No, I'd prefer a soft drink."

Wally smiled and said, "No problem. I have a cooler up-front with regular and Diet Coke, water and orange juice."

Almost stuttering, Harvey said, "I'll take a Diet Coke."

Handing him his drink, Wally said, "If you'd like something to read, I have The Wall Street Journal, Time, Sports Illustrated and USA Today."

As they were pulling away, Wally handed Harvey another laminated card.

"These are the stations I get and the music they play, if you'd like to listen to the radio."

And, as if that wasn't enough, Wally told Harvey that he had the air conditioning on and asked if the temperature was comfortable for him.

Then he advised Harvey of the best route to his destination for that time of day.

He also let him know that he'd be happy to chat and tell him about some of the sights or, if Harvey preferred, to leave him with his own thoughts.

Then Harvey said, "Tell me, Wally, have you always served customers like this?"

Wally smiled into the rear-view mirror. "No, not always. In fact, it's only been in the last two years. My first five years driving, I spent most of my time complaining like all the rest of the cabbies do.

"Then I decided to do things differently. I looked around at the other cabs and their drivers. The cabs were dirty, the drivers were unfriendly, and the customers were unhappy. So I decided to make some changes. I put in a few at a time. When my customers responded well, I did more."

"I take it that has paid off for you," Harvey said.

"It sure has," Wally replied. "In my first year I doubled my income from the previous year. This year I'll probably quadruple it. You were lucky to get me today. I don't sit at cabstands anymore.

"My customers call me for appointments on my cell phone or leave a message on my answering machine. If I can't pick them up myself I get a reliable cabbie friend to do it, and I take a piece of the action."

Wally was implementing Moments Of Truth, even though he didn't realise it!

This true story shows if Moments Of Truth can be so successful for a cab driver – it can work for any type of business – ESPECIALLY YOUR ACCOUNTANCY PRACTICE!

So how can you use this to your advantage? There are just three simple steps. Let's take a look at each one...

STEP 1: IDENTIFY THE KEY INTERACTIONS (MOMENTS) YOU HAVE WITH YOUR CLIENTS

Simply identify every single interaction you have with your clients. Here are the main ones...

- Car Parking (when a client comes to your office)
- Meetings At Client's Place Of Work
- Reception Area
- Meeting Room(s)
- Telephone Answering
- E-Mail
- Annual Review Meeting

STEP 2: CREATE AND SYSTEMISE THE POSITIVE EXPERIENCE AT EACH MOMENT

Now all you do is look at how you can maximise the interaction so that clients have a very positive experience with you at each interaction.

STEP 3: NOW ADD 'SPECIAL' MOMENTS OF TRUTH

What Moments Of Truth focuses on is the 'normal' interactions you have with your clients. The final piece of the jigsaw is to introduce NEW Moments Of Truth that heighten the experience for the prospect or client.

Here's a good example...

The Radisson chain of hotels is excellent at including 'Special' Moments Of Truth in the customer experience. Let's compare their approach to receiving new customers with the 'standard' service of other good hotels…

Moment Of Truth	Good Hotels	The Radisson
Check-In	Prompt, courteous welcome and efficient checking in.	Prompt, courteous welcome and efficient checking in, plus an acknowledgement that this is your first visit and a complimentary upgrade.
Entry Into Room	Maybe a complimentary bowl of fruit, bottle of water and a welcome message on the TV screen.	Welcome message on TV screen. A chocolate dessert with your name written in the chocolate sauce saying 'Welcome <Name>'. A book entitled 'This Is My Favourite…' with the favourite recipes from 100 of the UK's best chefs – and a complimentary note sticking out of the top saying: 'Dear <Name>, We believe this is your first visit to the Hotel. Please accept this book with our compliments' And finally a 'Welcome Card' from the Hotel Manager, personally addressed.

These are just two Moments Of Truth – but as you can see, by adding 'Special' Moments Of Truth to the experience, you really do set yourself apart!

Once you've tackled the more obvious points of contact, you don't have to stop there. Moments of Truth is all about focusing your practice on the expectations of your clients.

The two most frequent areas of compliance work, accounts production and tax returns, present the most common areas of client dissatisfaction, because the accountant thinks about these tasks from his or her perspective rather than from the client's.

From start to finish, these assignments offer multiple opportunities to apply Moments of Truth, and better every client's expectations every year.

So the question is – what 'Special Moments Of Truth' can you build into the firm when serving prospects and clients?

MANAGING YOUR CLIENT BASE

This final method to help retain more clients is, once again, extremely effective once you apply it to your firm.

Managing your client base is simple as long as you realise that not all clients are the same. Look at the table on the next page:

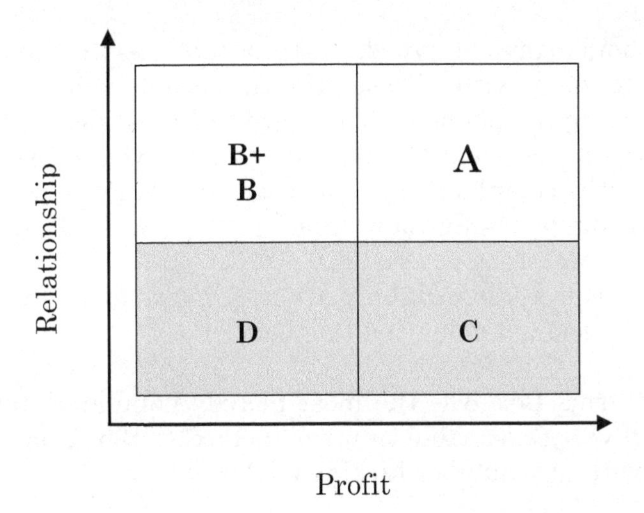

We are going to use this 'Boston Matrix' diagram to analyse your own client base.

The x-axis represents the financial value that the client has to your firm. The further along the axis, the more profitable they are. The y-axis measures the intangible, how much you enjoy having them as a client. The further up the scale, the better the relationship with them, and the greater respect they have for your staff and your firm as a whole.

With these four boxes you can now very easily categorise your clients...

Those in Box A are your best clients, very profitable for you and enjoyable to work with.

Those in Box B are the bread-and-butter clients. They are perfectly pleasant to work with, but don't make as much profit for you as you would wish. These tend to be compliance-focused clients. Within this group are the B+s.

These are businesses that you earmark as having potential. They don't spend enough with you yet but given the right handling, they could become A clients. They may be start-ups or businesses going through a period of change.

Box C holds an odd breed. As profitable as A clients but unpleasant to deal with. These are the people who everyone dreads picking up the phone to. These are the ones who make your heart sink when you send the bill out because you know what's coming next – the complaint. In some cases they may be polite and friendly with you, but bully your team.

Box D is even worse. Not only are they nasty to deal with but you don't make enough money on them either!

In most firms Box B is the most heavily populated, together with (hopefully) a reasonable number in Box A. Box C may have the odd one with any number lurking in Box D.

The problem with this set-up is that those in boxes C & D, whilst numerically in the minority, demand an unwarranted amount of your resources.

Their demands, lack of support and cooperation, complaints and general negativity drain your time and profit. As a result the 'nice' people in B and A, who don't jump up and down and pester you, are in danger of getting neglected. The focus of the firm ends up too much on those below the line.

The solution is to treat each box differently. Let us show you what we mean.

MANAGING YOUR CLIENTS

Let's start with Box D. You don't like them, they don't like you and you're not happy with the fees they eventually pay. Why are they still in <u>your</u> business? Having identified them, we can now remove them.

But, like any cull, this should be a controlled process that works to your advantage. Decide who goes when, in order to minimise the impact on your cash flow.

If you have a batch, then consider selling them to a firm more suitable for their needs. Ensure that any 'firing' letters are inoffensive and diplomatic to avoid the wrong message getting out in to the market place.

Crucially though, commit to removing all D clients.

Remember that the only difference between C and D clients is the profit that you make. That, at least, earns C clients the chance of a reprieve.

Meet with them, explain why the relationship isn't working for you and try to get to the root of the problem. Satisfactory resolution could mean another A client. No resolution means another D client to be handled out of the firm. No one stays in the C box.

How different does the firm look now that we only have A and B clients to look after? We've raised morale and freed up a significant amount of time. Now we can look after our clients properly.

Partners can now focus their time on their best A clients, ensuring their retention, increasing referrals and maximising the client value. In addition they can work with the B+s, nurturing their growth.

Let's not forget that the B clients are in the majority, and whilst nice people and easy clients to manage, they are not as profitable as we would wish.

The answer, therefore, is to ensure that they are predominantly looked after by a systemised process that meets their compliance needs, and is more effective at the fee level their budget allows.

The partners and managers control the system rather than trying to ad-hoc service the client. Much more profitable but of course with partners still in the background for support and handholding as required. It remains personal but much more effective.

2. Increasing Fees

One of the goals of your practice should be to increase your fees. No other strategy will be able to give you increased profit margins so quickly.

However, the only way you can increase your fees is by providing ADDED VALUE to your clients.

In our experience, many businesses charge too little for their products or services. The same goes for accountants!

There are only two factors to consider when setting your fees – value and profit. Concentrate on giving extraordinary levels of value – and profit will take care of itself!

There are two key factors to consider. Let's take a look at them...

Pricing & Adding Value

So how do you charge the right price for your services and how do you increase your fees by adding more value than the competition – ideally without having to change anything in your firm?

At the outset this may seem difficult and quite challenging, but once you understand how price and value work in harmony, and what you can do to ethically use it to your advantage, you'll be surprised at how easy it really is.

So let's first look at how to charge the perfect price for your services...

HOW TO CHARGE THE PERFECT PRICE FOR YOUR SERVICES

We can quite confidently say that you are **not** charging the right price (high enough) for your services. And when you consider that increasing your fees is *the quickest and easiest way to grow any practice* with increased profits, you're missing out on a huge opportunity.

Most accountants still use time-based billing to varying degrees. Whilst some still use it as the sole basis for the fee, most firms use their time budget as a means of calculating the theoretical fee. However, market assessment then takes over.

Here's how most accountants go about pricing their services...

- They calculate the theoretical bill based on time-cost records.
- They look at what their competitors charge.
- They decide 'where' they want their clients to view them (or what the client will stand) – are they 'low priced', 'middle of the road' or 'high end'?
- They then price their services based on the results of the three scenarios above but with market influence being dominant.

This is what's known as 'price positioning' and to a certain extent it does serve a purpose. But what it means is the firm bases their own fees on where they see themselves positioned in the market, in relation to what their competitors charge.

You might be saying to yourself, "Well, that's fine – isn't that how pricing should be done?" No it isn't!

This is a fundamental mistake. People rarely buy on price. Sure, there are a small percentage of people who buy the cheapest, but they are in the minority. Generally people buy based on 'VALUE', and 'price' and 'value' are two very different things!

Let us explain...

As a rule, people will automatically value your services more if they are priced higher (particularly for non-compliance services). The opposite is also true!

This may surprise you, but think about this simple example...

You go to two different restaurants on two different nights...

The first restaurant has a low-priced menu. Although you may think, "Great, a cheap meal", you will start having doubts about the quality of the food and the service – even before you enter the restaurant.

You keep these doubts hidden until you wait ten minutes to be greeted. You pass this off as "one of those things" but your doubts are starting to come to the fore.

You are seated at your table.

The table is still dirty from the previous diners. The waitress comes and takes your order. She has to keep asking you to repeat what you wanted. You really are now worrying. Not surprisingly, your order comes and it's all wrong, and so on.

The point here is, as soon as you saw the menu the doubts started, purely because the price was low. If you had a good experience then you'd be surprised, and you'd definitely go back.

The second point here is this – the restaurant should charge more if they serve you well and you have an enjoyable experience (the value is greater!).

The second restaurant you go to is different – very different…

The menu is very expensive. In fact, you've never been to a restaurant with prices so high. However, you automatically think, "It must be good if they charge these prices."

As long as you are treated exceptionally well and your food is also excellent, you would never quibble about the bill. The point is that, as soon as you saw the prices, you perceived the restaurant to be good even before you entered!

If you had a bad experience you'd never go back and pay those prices. The point here is this – although the restaurant charged high prices, they demonstrated to you with their service and food why they charge high prices. IN OTHER WORDS, THE VALUE THEY PROVIDED AT THE VERY LEAST MATCHED YOUR EXPECTATIONS.

It's exactly the same with your pricing. If you charge too low, your prospects and clients will automatically think you can't be that good. On the other hand, if you charge high prices you'd better make sure clients receive excellent value – because that's what they'll expect.

THE BIG QUESTION: HOW DO YOU ADD VALUE?

When you add the principle of 'value' to pricing, this is when you build 'elasticity' into your fees, which means you have a greater flexibility in your pricing. Here's an important note about 'value' and how it links to price…

The Ultimate Principle On Value And Price

As long as you provide excellent value – people will flock to your practice and pay handsomely for the privilege.

People often make the mistake of thinking that price is the main issue in the mind of their prospects or clients.

But what they're missing is this: if everyone is viewed by the prospect as 'the same' – i.e. companies don't take the time or effort to differentiate themselves from others and add considerable value – the only way the prospect can choose is based on price.

But when you add so much value to the firm – substantially more than your competitors – you leave the prospect with little choice.

And often they'll pay much more than anyone else. Why? Because you've added so much value!

Also, when a client decides to leave and turn to one of your competitors, they'll often say, 'Your price/fees are too high.' BUT WHAT THEY'RE REALLY SAYING IS THIS...

'Your services are not worth what you charge. I'm just not getting value for money!'

There's a big difference!

The diagrams on the following pages show the effect of value on price...

1. As you can see below, we have two similar but competing accountancy firms – Firm A and Firm B. Let's say that Firm A is a competitor and Firm B is YOUR Practice...

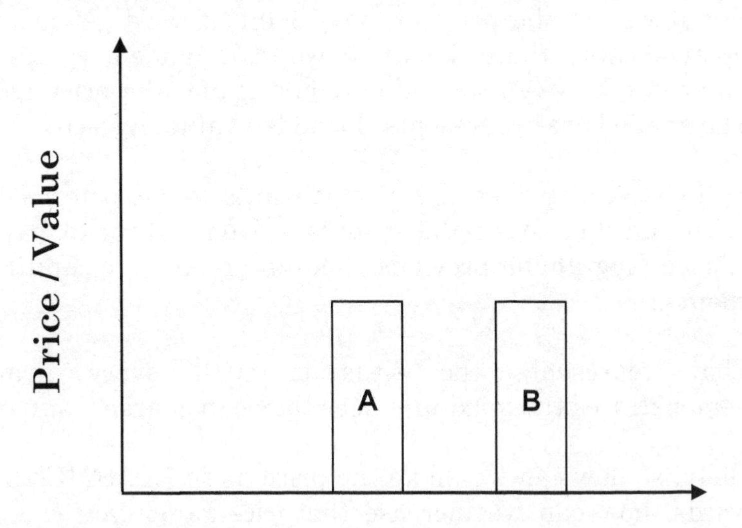

2. Let's assume that each firm has a similar price structure for its services and similar value attached to them...

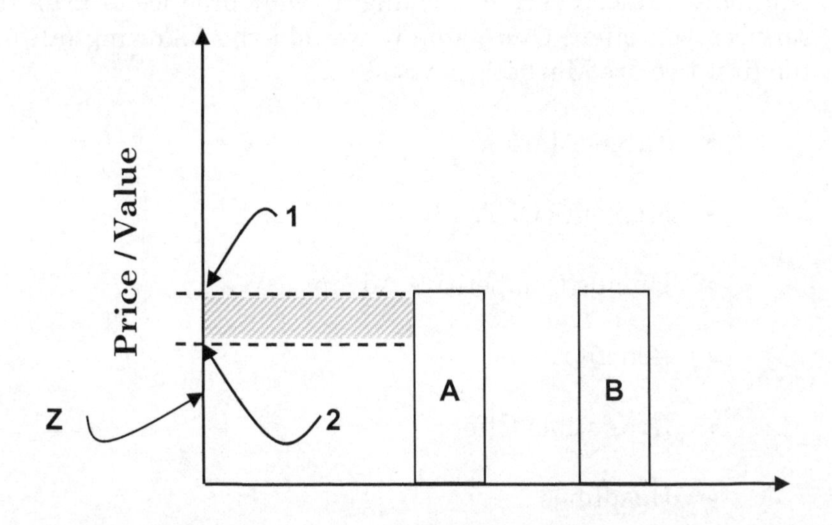

So at the moment point '1' (shown below) is the maximum value of each service offered by each firm. So if we look at pricing either service, we are unlikely to get many sales if we price the services above point '1' because the perceived value is lower than the price.

But if we set the price at, say, point '2' we'd get more sales because now there is what we call 'added value' – the difference between the value (point 1) and the price (point 2). The shaded area represents the added value. Agreed?

So Firm A may take the view it wants to compete heavily on price and therefore reduces its fees even further to, say, point 'Z' (see diagram on previous page) in an effort to capture more clients.

That represents the situation with every firm and demonstrates the maximum fees they can charge – agreed?

Okay, so how can we make the price more ELASTIC? In other words, how can we increase the price range you can charge clients?

3. That's right – we add more value. How do you think we can add more value WITHOUT changing your practice or even the services you offer? Quite simply we add the following (all but the first two are Marketing Assets)...

- Target Market
- Moments Of Truth
- Unique Competitive Advantage
- Benefits
- Irresistible Offer
- Headlines
- Guarantee/Risk Reversal
- Social Proof

These elements are at point 'C' on the diagram below. Now let's see how our diagram looks...

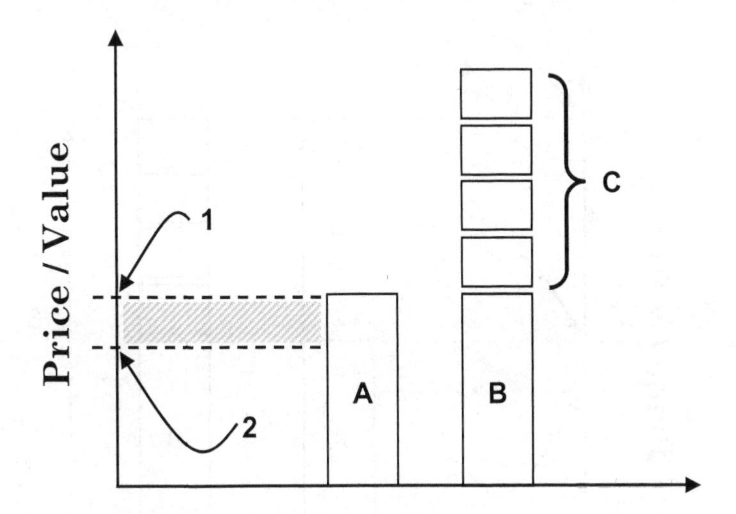

As you can see, we're adding value over and above what the competition are doing.

Now look at the price elasticity (3 – see diagram on next page). You could price your services right up to point 4 now. But would you get many sales at point 4? No you wouldn't, because at that point there's no added value. But what if you priced your services at point 5 – would you get many sales? Yes you would.

That's the power of adding value and creating price elasticity.

4. So what about a price-sensitive market? We explained earlier why, in most circumstances, a price-sensitive market isn't actually the case. But let's say at the moment you don't want (or you're nervous) to increase your fees because you believe you're in a price-sensitive market (many accountants think this!).

So all you do is keep your fees the same. But now, after adding all this value, who do you think gets most of the sales? That's right – YOU do. Why? Because point 6 (see below) represents the added value your firm (B) has over the competition (A).

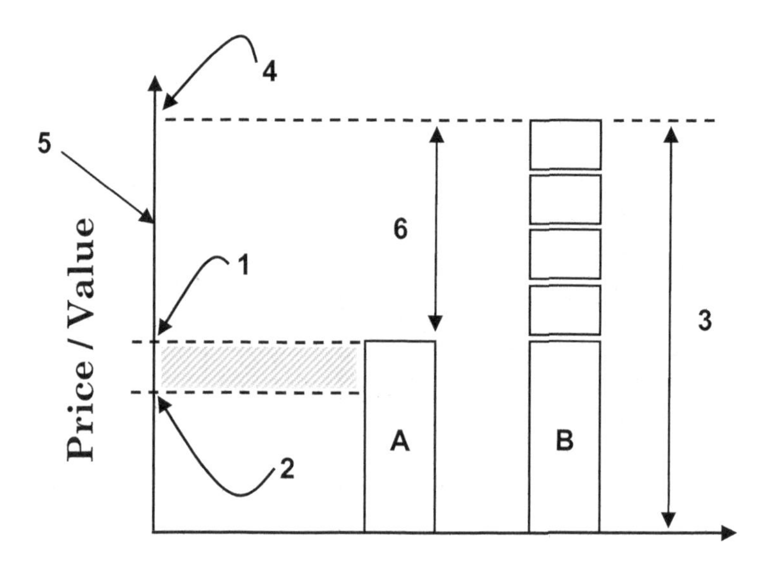

So that's how you can increase your prices, or maintain your existing prices, and STILL generate more clients and sales just by using the Marketing Assets, Target Market and Moments Of Truth to add value to your firm.

Base your pricing on *value* rather than on price and you'll be surprised how much more money you'll make!

3. SELLING MORE SERVICES

Now we need to get your clients buying more frequently from you. In other words – getting them to buy more services from you.

Traditionally accountants are uncomfortable when it comes to selling 'business development services' (we call these 'Building A Better Business Services').

...and here's why most firms struggle to effectively sell them...

1. **NOT PACKAGED RIGHT:** The accountant tells the client what the service is but it's not 'packaged' correctly, making it hard to buy and less appealing.

2. **NO ADDED VALUE:** Just as we have highlighted above, there is no added value communicated to the client.

3. **NO OFFER:** When the services are offered to clients there's no offer making them irresistible to buy.

4. **NOT SOLD:** Remember when selling the service – you must adhere to the 5 Ms Of Marketing Your Accountancy Firm.

5. **MISSED OPPORTUNITIES:** The opportunities to sell these services are all around you, yet are often missed because you just don't 'see them'.

So, it's hardly surprising that these additional high-profit services generate a small percentage of the overall fee income in most firms – yet the opposite should be true – and can be if you focus on all these elements.

Black & Grey Accountants

Black & Grey of course fully appreciate the impact a small increase in fees can have on their profits. So they decide to increase fees by 10% for the next 12 months. This is a good strategy. However, because they aren't adding value to their services, this increase (although relatively easy with new clients) is likely to be met with disdain from a number of existing clients. How can they justify the increase?

AFG Accountants LLP

"Moving the firm to a value-based practice is by far the best and easiest way to maximise fees and to increase GRFs. Retaining clients, increasing fees and selling more services are the three things you can focus on to increase the monetary value of every client.

"Yes it takes time to put all these strategies into practice, but once they're in place they will keep working for you month after month.

"Once again, the great thing about all these strategies is they cost very little to apply and they work immediately once they're in place."

KEY SUMMARY & ACTION POINTS

1. To maximise the monetary value of your clients you have to focus on just three key areas: (1) Improving Client Retention, (2) Increasing Fees, and (3) Selling More Services.

2. To improve client retention you need to create your unique competitive advantage, apply Moments Of Truth and manage your client base effectively.

3. To increase fees you have to add value.

4. To sell more services you have to...

- package your services so they're more attractive to your clients

- add value

- create an enticing offer

- use the 5 Ms Of Marketing Your Accountancy Firm

- grasp the opportunities

AGENDA ITEM 13

13. ACTIONS & IMPLEMENTATION PLAN

INTRODUCTION

The first 12 agenda points cover the steps you need to take to quickly grow your practice. This section looks at the actions you need to take and the implementation process.

Just like any board meeting or partner meeting, if the actions agreed at the meeting aren't carried out – the practice won't move forward. The same can be said about this book.

It's taking action (massive action) that will get you the results you seek. So in this section we look at everything that needs to be put in place across the '5 Ms Of Marketing Your Accountancy Firm' and the '4 Practice Multipliers'. The details on how you carry out each task have been shown throughout the book.

ACTIONS – 5 MS OF MARKETING YOUR ACCOUNTANCY FIRM

Market

- Analyse your existing client base. Look for the type of clients that generate 60-80% of your GRFs. These are the low-hanging fruit and represent the easiest clients to acquire.

- Look for specific target markets that you already have expertise in. The more credibility and social proof in these markets you have, the better.

- Use the target market characteristics detailed earlier. These will help you identify the best target market(s) for your firm.

- Again, using the target market characteristics, write down clearly the definition of your target market(s).

- If you want to change the profile of clients you acquire, you need to do it gradually. Acquisition of clients which represent big jumps in their size, compared to existing clients, is especially hard to achieve.

Message

- Create your own Unique Perceived Benefit (unique competitive advantage). Remember, it not only has to be unique, it also has to be highly desired by your clients and potential clients (the target market).

- Convert all the features of your services and the delivery of them into benefits. People buy on emotion (benefits) and back up their decision with logic (features).

- Create an offer that's irresistible to your target market. Free Special Reports help position you as an expert and immediately set you apart from the competition. You must 'sell' the meeting so the prospect is excited and more than happy to spend time with you.

- Every message and marketing piece must have a headline that grabs the attention of the target market. Your company name is NOT a headline.

- Create a number of powerful guarantees that minimise the risk clients take when using your services. Guarantees are also excellent sales converting strategies.

- Establish a sales barrier demolition to further differentiate your firm and attract the target market to you like a magnet.

- Once you've created an irresistible offer together with your guarantee and sales barrier demolition, you need to list the reasons why you are making these things available. Otherwise the target market will believe what you're offering is too good to be true.

- The more proof and credibility you provide as part of your message – the more clients you'll acquire. You can't have enough testimonials and other sources of credibility.

- People are silently begging to be led. Therefore you must tell them what to do. You achieve this with what we call a call to action.

Media

- Select your media categories (Published Media, Direct Marketing Media, E-Media) to deliver your message to the target market. Tests have proven that combining all three media categories gets the best results.

Moment

- People are constantly moving 'in' and 'out' of buying mode because of their ever-changing circumstances. You use this to your advantage by contacting the target market at least six times a year (but the more the better). Therefore you need to create at least 6 marketing pieces a year to communicate your message to the target market.

Method

- Identifying your media categories will help you decide on your marketing pieces to use to deliver your message to the target market. To get results, your marketing pieces need to stand out and rise above the clutter. Remember, you are not just competing against other accountants looking to acquire your target market; you are also competing against EVERY other business targeting the same people. The marketing pieces that grab attention are the ones that get looked at – increasing your chances of success considerably.

ACTIONS – THE 4 PRACTICE MULTIPLIERS

More Enquiries By Referral

- Create a referral system for clients and for third-party referral sources (IFAs, banks, solicitors, etc.). For the system to work effectively you need a sought-after unique competitive advantage, an incentive and an effective method for communicating the referral system. Without all these things in place your referral system won't be as successful as it should be.

More Enquiries By General Marketing

- Having identified the media categories you'll be using to reach your target market, you should have a list of a number of general marketing activities you should be undertaking. You now need to create each marketing piece ready for launch. Remember to monitor the results of all your marketing and test small when you have no history of results.

Converting More Enquiries Into Sales (Sales Conversion)

- Create and apply a sales conversion system which helps you to convert more enquiries into clients. It should consist of at least 7 points of contact (most people buy after 7 contacts) and include sales conversion strategies such as guarantees and social proof.

Maximising Fees From Clients

- Improve your client retention by (1) applying Moments Of Truth across your practice and (2) managing your client base by segmenting clients into the 5 key categories (A, B, B+, C, D).

- Increase fees by adding value.
- Sell more services by (1) making each of your services more desirable (packaging them so they are more appealing), (2) adding value, (3) creating a compelling offer for each service that makes it difficult for clients to refuse (use the 5 Ms for each service), and (4) identify the regular opportunities (annual client meetings, a cry for help, etc.) to sell other services to clients.

IMPLEMENTATION

Clearly all this represents a significant amount of work. There's no escaping the fact. But you have to put the effort in if you are genuinely serious about growing your practice.

Amongst all your other work commitments, you need to put aside one or two days a week to focus on growing the practice. That's a lot of time for anyone – especially a partner of the firm. But if you don't put this amount of effort in, we can assure you your targets won't be reached.

And in many cases that's where the problem lies. Accountants are so busy working in the business that finding time to work ON the business is challenging to say the least.

Without doubt, managing your client base as we have described will help free up more time. But you have to make a time commitment to growing the practice. If you keep doing what you're doing, you're going to get what you've always got. So something has to change. You have to change and prioritise growing the firm.

We recommend you block out your time to focus on growing the practice. This means putting 'pretend' appointments in your diary that you treat like real appointments.

Once you've done this you need to start tackling the actions we've highlighted. Systematically going through each action point is your best approach.

Only one person is going to change your firm....YOU.

This is clearly true for a sole practitioner but is just as relevant for you if you are in a multiple partner firm. It may be a slower process to turn around an oil tanker than a single-handed yacht, but in both cases the process starts by an individual turning the wheel. Leave it to someone else and you carry on as you are.

BLACK & GREY ACCOUNTANTS

Black & Grey have agreed that one of the partners will focus on growing the practice. Everyone acknowledges that his task is going to be challenging and the meeting concludes with the statement, 'Just try and get done what you can'. It pleases the partner in charge of growing the firm because now he has a 'get out'. Nevertheless the meeting finishes on a high and everyone is looking forward to seeing the progress made over the next 6 months.

AFG ACCOUNTANTS LLP

"As you can now see, growing an accountancy firm isn't easy. There are dozens of things that need to be implemented. Dedicating time to creating, launching, testing and improving each element is especially time-consuming. But it is valuable work that has to be done.

"But as you know, there is a better way – a much better way.

"That's why we created the 'Accountants Growth Programme'. Everything is already done for you. It's been created so even a junior member of staff can implement the entire system.

"All you now need to do is appoint a partner responsible for overseeing and managing the implementation of the system, and a junior member of staff to do the implementation. It really is that simple."

Agenda Item 14

14. Date Of Next Progress Meeting

Introduction

Both firms, although they review progress at each monthly partner meeting, agree to review the overall results in 6 months' time.

The partner responsible for the growth of each firm will present the results. John will present for Black & Grey and Sarah will present for AFG Accountants LLP.

Progress Meeting

Results So Far

Introduction

The results of both firms over a six-month period show a completely different picture. Where relevant, our comments are in the grey boxes. Take a look...

Black & Grey Accountants (By John)

Summary Of Results

- Enquiries Generated: 10 (6 by referral, 4 by general marketing).

> ***Our Comments...***
>
> *This is a typical volume of enquiries for any good practice. These numbers, though, are low, especially when combined with the new clients they have generated. If you're serious about growing your firm this level of enquiries simply isn't enough, especially when you take into account client losses.*
>
> *Clearly the level of enquiries you need is dependent on the number of clients you need to acquire to hit your acquisition targets for the next 12 months.*

- New Clients Acquired: 5 (4 through referral, 1 through general marketing).

Our Comments:

As you'd expect, the conversion of referral-based enquiries (66%) is significantly higher than general marketing enquiries (25%). Both these conversion rates are typical but are far too low for our liking.

You should be aiming for a conversion on referral enquiries of around 80-90% and 60-80% on general marketing enquiries. These results are achievable when you implement a sales conversion system.

- Clients Lost: 10 (6 moved to another accountant, 3 went bust, 1 sold).

Our Comments:

It's interesting that most firms – even the good firms – don't believe they have a client attrition (client losses) problem. Of course there's little you can do about sales and bankruptcies, but you should strive to have zero defections through unhappy clients.

Black & Grey, in the last six months, have started to see losses increase. Again this is typical. Most businesses have spent the last two years fire-fighting and as the economy slowly improves they are becoming more discerning and expecting much more from their accountant.

You must deliver added value and exceptional service levels otherwise you too will suffer increasing client losses, just as Black & Grey are experiencing.

- Average Fee Income From New Clients: £1,450 (per year).

Our Comments:

On its own this figure is difficult to interpret; however, your overall objective with every business client is to increase their monetary value.

- Average Fee Income From Lost Clients: £1,900 (per year).

Our Comments:

Black & Grey have not only lost 10 clients – they've lost 10 good clients. It's interesting that when clients leave, they say 'your fees are too high' but in reality this often means 'you're not providing enough value for money'.

Do NOT fall into the trap of thinking your fees are too high – they rarely are. You should be thinking 'how can we add value to the relationships we have with our clients' and not 'how do we cut our fees'.

- Increase/Decrease In Average Fees Of Existing Clients: No change.

Our Comments:

The net loss in income from client gains and client losses is £11,750. This was tempered by the strategy to increase fees 10% across all clients (a good one – but more effective if value had been added prior to the increase).

Things are okay, but Black & Grey are barely holding their own. If you're standing still, in reality you're not – you're going backwards. Again, if you're looking to move your own practice on, you cannot let it get into this position!

Review

These first six months have been challenging on many fronts. The economy has obviously played a significant part in client acquisitions and losses, but I have found it hard to implement a number of our initiatives due to a lack of time, not helped by having to fire-fight with existing clients.

I have been relatively pleased with the number of referrals we have had (6) that have converted into clients (4) although the number of new clients (1) through general marketing has not reached my expectations.

Referrals have increased because we started asking for them, although this has been a little bit 'hit and miss' since we find it awkward and difficult to ask for referrals.

Perhaps more disturbing is our number of client losses (10) which, for only the second time in our history, have been more than client gains (5). Plus, the majority of our losses are from long-term clients who have decided to change accountants. This has resulted in an approximate overall loss of income of almost £12,000, although our 10% increase of fees has worked well (even though it may have contributed to some of the client defections!) and means there is no overall net decrease in fee income (we have stayed roughly the same).

Elements Implemented

Market

- We agreed a target market of £2m - £5m.

> ***Our Comments:***
>
> *This target market is challenging because it's a big jump from their 'bread-and-butter' clients.*

Notice only one new client was gained from general marketing, which suggests two things: (1) the target market is wrong and (2) the marketing used was ineffective.

This is a common occurrence, especially with the target market. As we said earlier, if you're not happy with the current size and scope of your clients, you cannot quickly move to much larger clients – you have to make small jumps in size. Yes it takes longer, but at least you will get there!

Message

- Unique Perceived Benefit: Fixed fees.

Our Comments:

Offering 'fixed fees' isn't unique. It's definitely something you should be offering, but it isn't going to make your target market sit up and think 'wow'.

- Benefits: Proactive, personal service, value, reliability, support, service second to none, save tax and maximise profits.

Our Comments:

None of these things are benefits – they are all features. Yet these terms and phrases are used extensively by 95% of accountancy firms.

No one (and we repeat 'no one') gets excited by any of these things and you're deluding yourself if you think otherwise.

- Irresistible Offer: Free no-obligation meeting.

Our Comments:

Gary Halbert, the late, great copywriter, said you should imagine your prospect as a huge sloth of a man who's lying on his bed watching his favourite TV programme.

It's going to take a herculean effort for him to pick up the phone and request a meeting. Therefore your offer has to be so exciting, so different and so valuable to him that he actually drags himself away from his favourite TV programme, and up from his bed to make the call.

If your offer is like Black & Grey, you've got problems.

- Headline: Black & Grey.

Our Comments:

We know you're proud of your firm. We know it took a lot of blood, sweat and tears to get it to where it is today. But your clients and potential clients don't care about you. They care about what you can do for them. Your name as a headline is THE worst headline you could use.

We have a good test for the quality of a headline. Imagine the headline is the entire ad. You can only add the words 'Call now for further information' after the headline. When you read the ad it has to make you think, 'Yes I would call this business'.

If it doesn't, then it's back to the drawing board. Obviously 'Black & Grey, call now for further information' doesn't pass this simple test!

- Guarantee: None.

Our Comments:

Although guarantees are becoming more popular with a small number of accountants, they are still rarely used.

Remember, guarantees demonstrate to the client that you stand behind your promises. They work very well at the point of purchase as a powerful sales conversion strategy and can also double up as a uniqueness in their own right. You omit them at your peril.

- Sales Barrier Demolition: None.

Our Comments:

The multi-stage guarantee has the capacity to transform your practice overnight. Black & Grey, like so many firms, don't appreciate the value of this little-known tactic.

Admittedly, sales barrier demolition is never easy to create, but once you've got something in place you will be astounded by its effectiveness.

- Reasons Why: None.

Our Comments:

You don't need reasons why if you don't have an irresistible offer, a powerful guarantee or a sales barrier demolition strategy in place. Reasons why are necessary when your offer may sound sensational to the target market.

- Social Proof: Two testimonials.

> ***Our Comments:***
>
> *At least Black & Grey understand the value of using testimonials in their message. But, like everything we advise and recommend, there are right and wrong ways of doing it. Not putting the full name and the name of the business at the end of the testimonial is common – yet will immediately cast doubt over everything you say.*

- Call To Action: None.

> ***Our Comments:***
>
> *Just putting a phone number at the end of your marketing piece doesn't constitute a call to action. You have to build in something that reduces procrastination (stimulator) and summarise the offer.*

Media

- Direct Marketing Media, Published Media and E-Media.

> ***Our Comments:***
>
> *This is good. Black & Grey are using all three media categories to reach the target market.*

Moment

- The same letter was mailed twice.

Our Comments:

This is a very common approach to contacting the target market. In fact, Black & Grey have gone one better than most firms in that at least they sent the letter out twice.

Of course you can get lucky with this approach, whereby you 'catch' a few prospects at the right time, but by contacting the target market more frequently (at least 6 times a year) the 'luckier' you'll get.

This is a very basic phenomenon that is so easy to capitalise upon – yet so few do.

Method

- Lead generation letter, website and Yellow Pages ad.

Our Comments:

Black & Grey correctly decided to use all three media categories; however, the website, letter and ad they used were all very typical. Very samey. Very 'accountant-like'.

None of them rise above the clutter. None of them have a complete message. None of them work anywhere near as well as they should (see examples on next pages).

BLACK & GREY'S LETTER

B&G
Black & Grey
Accountants

<Name and Address>

<Date>

Dear <Name>,

I am writing to introduce our firm to you. Black & Grey are an established firm of accountants specialising in helping businesses with their financing and accounting needs.

Over the last ten years we have helped many businesses with our proactive and personal service. We are a partner led practice and our service is second to none. Our approach to fixed price quotes is always popular and ensures you always know how much you will pay.

Here is what some of our clients have to say about us:

> "I have used Black & Grey for over five years on a business and personal basis. Their professionalism and competence in handling my affairs has been exemplary. They adopt a 'can-do' attitude and are prepared to go the extra mile to satisfy a client. Having used large national accountancy firms in the past, the level of service I receive from Black & Grey is most gratifying and I know the answer to any query I have is only a telephone call away. I have no hesitation in recommending them to anyone seeking a caring, personal and professional service. Nice people to do business with and they make life much less taxing!" - *AS - Stourbridge*

> "Black & Grey provide sound advice and guidance and have helped me to get our organisation on a really sound financial basis with excellent systems and advice. We made good profits before our relationship with them; however, we have now been able to look at other ways to manage our budgets to increase our profits without affecting our business image." - *PN - Gloucester*

We offer a full range of compliance and support services including audit, accounts, tax planning, payroll and bookkeeping at very competitive prices. We also offer free telephone advice and support.

We would like to take this opportunity to meet with you. We offer a free no-obligation meeting. Simply phone us **on 0123 456 789** and we'll be happy to discuss how we can help.

If you would like any further information, please do not hesitate to contact us on the number below.

Yours sincerely,

For and on behalf of Black & Grey

Black & Grey Accountants

Any Street, Any Town, Any City. Any Postcode
Tel: 0123 456 7890 Fax: 0123 456 7891
Web: blackandgreyaccts.co.uk

BLACK & GREY'S YELLOW PAGES AD

B&G

Black & Grey Chartered Accountants

- Business Planning
- Raising Finance
- Profit Improvement
- Tax Advice
- Bookkeeping & Payroll
- Audit & Accountancy
- VAT & Income Tax Advice
- Start-Ups
- Self-Employed
- Partnerships
- Limited Companies
- Self-Assessment
- Fixed Quotes
- Established over 10 years

For a proactive and personal service, one that helps you save tax and maximise profits, look no further...

For your free no-obligation meeting phone

0123 456 7890

Black & Grey Chartered Accountants
Any Street, Any Town, Any City. Any Postcode
Tel: 0123 456 7890 Fax: 0123 456 7891
Web: blackandgreyaccts.co.uk

Black & Grey's Website Home Page

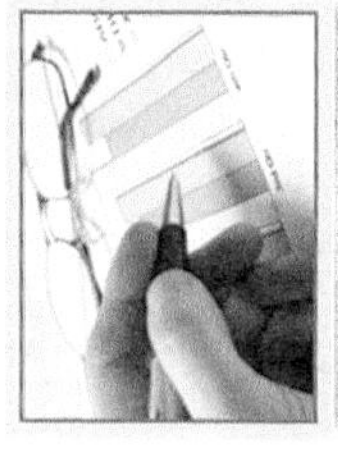

ACTIONS – THE 4 PRACTICE MULTIPLIERS

More Enquiries By Referral

- Partners and managers were tasked with asking clients for referrals.

> ***Our Comments:***
>
> *This is not a system. In most firms, partners and managers are reluctant to ask for referrals as they find it awkward and even embarrassing. Therefore results will at best be hit and miss.*
>
> *You need to put something in place that takes away this awkwardness and also ensures a high take-up rate from not only clients, but also third-party referral sources.*

More Enquiries By General Marketing

- The website was already in place. A Yellow Pages ad was created and placed and a one-page lead generation letter was created.

> ***Our Comments:***
>
> *Black & Grey have restricted their growth by NOT using more marketing strategies across each media category.*
>
> *Your aim should be to have at least a dozen marketing strategies spread across the media categories. If every one of these strategies was working well for you, just think about what that would mean to your practice.*

Converting More Enquiries Into Sales (Sales Conversion)

- No changes were implemented here.

Our Comments:

Black & Grey's conversion rates are not industry leading. They are very typical, but could be so much better. The combination of having a sales conversion system in place alongside a unique competitive advantage, and a host of other strategies we have highlighted throughout this book, would transform conversion rates.

Remember, improving the conversion of enquiries into clients doesn't cost a single penny!

Maximising Fees From Clients

- The 10% overall increase in fees was executed and helped to steady the ship as client losses exceeded client gains.

Our Comments:

Black & Grey's strategy of a 10% increase across all clients was a wise move and demonstrates that most firms don't charge enough.

However, without adding value to the relationship they have with clients, this is a dangerous ploy and may be responsible for a number of client losses.

AFG ACCOUNTANTS LLP

Summary Of Results

- Enquiries Generated: 38 (22 by referral, 16 by general marketing).

> ***Our Comments...***
>
> *This is more like it! If you're looking to grow, you have to accept that generating enquiries is the lifeblood of the practice.*
>
> *You have to be prolific in this area if you want to dominate your competition.*

- New Clients Acquired: 27 (17 through referral, 10 through general marketing).

> ***Our Comments:***
>
> *Conversion of referrals is approaching 80% and conversion of general marketing is just over 60%. Both these results are getting close to industry-best figures, but there is still room for improvement.*

- Clients Lost: 6 (2 moved to another accountant, 3 went bust, 1 sold).

> ***Our Comments:***
>
> *There's nothing you can do about four of the six clients lost. But losing just two clients is a good result in this economic climate.*

- Average Fee Income From New Clients: £2,350 (per year).

Our Comments:

Notice the difference here compared to Black & Grey. Almost £1,000 more per year per client.

- Average Fee Income From Lost Clients: £1,900 (per year).

Our Comments:

These were also two good clients lost, but notice that new clients are generating more fee income!

- Increase/Decrease In Average Fees Of Existing Clients: 12% increase.

Our Comments:

This is a great result. A 12% increase on top of the increase in overall fees through new client acquisition is a significant step forward.

Review

We are a good firm, so I openly admit I was a little sceptical about using the 'Accountants Growth Programme' in the beginning. But as we all agreed, we needed to do something different if we wanted to see a better result than our previous 12 months.

I have to say the first 6 months' results have shown how successful the programme is for us.

We appointed Rachel to implement the system. She spends half a day a week on the programme and I oversee it. I would say I spend about half a day a month on it, so time simply hasn't been an issue.

Because everything is done for us and each element comes with simple and step-by-step instructions, Rachel just gets on with it. Any questions (although few and far between) are handled by AFG so I don't even get involved in that.

The whole process has really opened my eyes to what we can achieve as a firm. We have, through the years, all been frustrated in the knowledge that we deserve to be doing better, and now we have the solution.

I would also say that in the early months we were a little worried about the style of the marketing. In fact, we held back on a few things but once we saw results in other areas, we just put these thoughts behind us and now we just do it.

So, in summary, we have acquired 27 new clients. 17 through referral and 10 through general marketing. These new clients have an anticipated average fee income of £2,350 which is well above our existing client average fee.

Client losses are also down. We lost 6 in the period but only 2 left to other firms. Again we should be pleased with this.

Probably the best news is that we have increased fee income by 12% and new client acquisitions have increased fees by another £60,000.

Elements Implemented

Market

- After carefully analysing our client base, we decided to target owner-managed businesses with a turnover of £400k - £1m. Most of our GRFs come from businesses with a turnover of £200k - £750k, but we wanted to target slightly larger clients.

Our Comments:

The target market choice is sensible. Yes they decided to target slightly larger firms, but the jump in size is relatively small. Small enough not to matter to any potential new client. Their results reinforce that the target market choice has been successful.

Message

- Unique Perceived Benefit: Free access for every client to what has been described as "the world's leading marketing and business growth system of its kind".

Our Comments:

If you assembled 100 business owners (clients and non-clients) in a room and gave them one wish for their businesses, what do you think most of them would ask for?

At least 90% of them would want more customers or at least more sales from existing customers. Yes, they all want to minimise the tax they pay and maximise profits (this is where you come in), but 95% of their challenges or problems can be overcome with more sales from new and/or existing customers.

So because AFG Accountants LLP are members of the Accountants Growth Programme, all their business clients get ***free*** *access to the 'Business Growth System'.*

Steve has developed the system over a 15-year period and it has been used successfully in 46 different countries and in over 250 industries. It is responsible for generating millions of pounds worldwide and sells for £1,175.

The Business Growth System forms the unique perceived benefit because it is highly desirable for clients and we only allow one accountant in each area to join the Accountants Growth Programme – therefore providing genuine uniqueness to each member.

Put yourself in your client's or your target market's shoes for a second.

What would you think if your accountant offered this system to help you grow your own businesses? To say you'd be impressed would be an understatement.

- Benefits: Many.

Our Comments:

Because everything in the Accountants Growth Programme is already done for you, all the benefits are automatically included in EVERY marketing piece.

- Irresistible Offer: Free no-obligation meeting with clear reasons why the meeting is worthwhile and a free special report titled '27 Common Financial & Marketing Mistakes And How To Overcome Them'.

Our Comments:

The special report (already done for you) reinforces your expertise and since you could be the only firm offering it in your area – again it acts as a point of difference. The meeting is described in detail, in terms of the benefits it will bring to the prospective client, alongside a few other secret tactics which only members have access to.

All in all, getting meetings with the target market is made much easier with this approach.

- Headline: Many.

> ***Our Comments:***
>
> *Once again every marketing piece in the Accountants Growth programme comes with powerful headlines that stop your target market dead in their tracks.*

- Guarantee: Yes.

> ***Our Comments:***
>
> *We give members a choice of several guarantees to add to their practice. Each has been tested 'in the heat of battle' (like everything in the programme) to ensure success.*

- Sales Barrier Demolition: Yes.

> ***Our Comments:***
>
> *The programme comes with a number of options for a sales barrier demolition strategy. You just choose the one that suits you and your firm best.*

- Reasons Why: Yes.

> ***Our Comments:***
>
> *Because the offer, the guarantee and the sales barrier demolition are all powerful, each one comes with a simple explanation on why you are offering all these things – immediately allaying any fears the target market may have.*

- Social Proof: Many.

> ***Our Comments:***
>
> *We of course can't provide you with client testimonials, but what we do give you is a very simple one-page letter called 'Testimonials By The Dozen' which you send to your clients.*
>
> *Within a few days you'll have dozens of great testimonials you can use in all your marketing.*

- Call To Action: Yes.

> ***Our Comments:***
>
> *Every marketing piece in the programme (60+ of them) comes with its own powerful call to action. Once again you don't have to do anything!*

Media

- Direct Marketing Media, Published Media and E-Media.

> ***Our Comments:***
>
> *Since our advice is to use all three media categories the Accountants Growth programme covers all three.*

Moment

- Four different 'Ready-To-Go Client Attraction Mailing Pieces' were used.

Our Comments:

The Accountants Growth Programme comes with 12 tested and highly effective mailing pieces for you to send every other month to the target market.

Method

- Client Attraction Mailing Pieces (x4), website landing page, Yellow Pages ad, referral system for clients and third-party referral sources, press releases, networking scripts, Google AdWords, past client reactivation letter, past prospect letter (see a few examples on the next pages).

Our Comments:

As you can see, AFG Accountants LLP have been very active. In 'normal' circumstances this level of activity simply couldn't be achieved. But because everything is ready-to-go it takes very little time and effort to activate any of the 60+ methods in the programme.

Also, it's worth pointing out at this stage that all the marketing pieces have been rigorously tested. You don't have to do any testing. You can activate each marketing strategy with complete peace of mind.

...and remember Rachel is 'only' an office junior. She has no experience in sales and marketing – and doesn't need any to effectively implement the programme.

Client Attraction Mailing Piece: The Invitation

Client Attraction Mailing Piece: The Comic

CLIENT ATTRACTION MAILING PIECE: THE X-RAY

Is Your Existing Accountant Giving You A Headache?

If so, I have good news... Our 'treatment' of this common condition is simple. We give our clients exactly what they want and believe me no other accountant in Stourbridge can permanently cure this ailment like we can.

For example, we have invested £thousands so our clients get FREE access to what has been described as "the world's leading business growth and marketing system". The system itself has generated tens of millions of pounds worldwide for companies in over 250 different industries. Better still it's a UK system; built, developed and improved over a 15 year period. But that's not all...

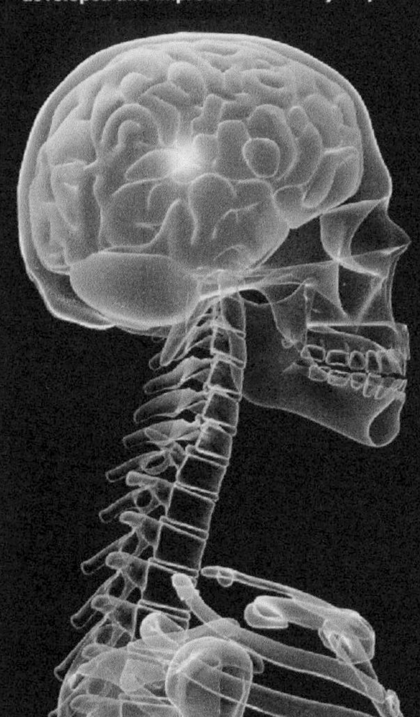

We specialise in helping small and medium-sized owner managed businesses to become financially sound whilst minimising the amount of tax they pay and we do it with a performance guarantee no one else dares to match.

So if you'd like instant relief from your headache, all you have to do is arrange your FREE no-obligation initial meeting. Simply phone us on 0123 456 7654 or alternatively complete our online form here...

www.<specific landing page with only a form on>.co.uk.

Plus, we guarantee the meeting will be one of the best meetings you have this year. In fact if you think we've wasted your time we'll gladly hand over a cheque for £100 to your favourite charity. We can't be fairer than that!

Copyright ©
AFG Accountants LLP
<Address and Postcode>
<Tel Number>

YELLOW PAGES AD

"WARNING: Don't Contact Another Accountant Until You've Read This"

Are you fed up with accountants that just do accounts? If you're like most people you're not alone. You see not only do we **improve your financial performance,** we also help you to **grow your business**.

In fact, we've invested in an initiative called '**The Business Growth Programme**' and as a result ALL our clients have completely FREE access to *'The Business Growth System'*. The system itself has generated tens of millions of pounds worldwide for *start-ups*, **small** and medium-sized companies in over 250 different industries. Better still, it's a UK **system**, improved over a 15 year period.

So now our unique services help you to *improve your cash flow*, grow your business and **keep more of the money you make**.

So if you're looking for an accountant with a difference, who genuinely cares about the financial health and growth of your business, call us now on **0123 456 7654** to arrange your FREE **initial meeting**.

AAAAAA **AFG Accountants LLP**

<Address> <Postcode> <Tel Number> <Main Landing Page>

ACTIONS – THE 4 PRACTICE MULTIPLIERS

More Enquiries By Referral

- The 'Client Referral System' and the 'Third-Party Referral System' were activated.

> ***Our Comments:***
>
> *The Accountants Growth Programme includes two referral systems already done for you. Included in your membership is a bespoke DVD tailored to your firm which promotes you and the uniqueness (the Business Growth System).*
>
> *This is a very effective way to communicate your uniqueness and promote the referral programme. And, of course, these systems take away any uncomfortable feelings you may have when asking for referrals (you don't have to ask – the system does it for you).*

More Enquiries By General Marketing

- Client Attraction Mailing Pieces (x4), website landing page (working in harmony with the existing website), Yellow Pages ad, referral system for clients and third-party referral sources, press releases, networking scripts, Google AdWords, Past Client Reactivation Letter, Past Prospect Letter.

> ***Our Comments:***
>
> *There are many more general marketing activities that could have been implemented over the 6-month period, but the key to all this is to implement at your own speed.*

Remember, with growth come other challenges (like greater workload on staff) so you need to be mindful of how much you want to grow and how quickly.

Converting More Enquiries Into Sales (Sales Conversion)

- The Sales Conversion System was implemented.

Our Comments:

The Accountants Growth Programme comes with a very successful and easy-to-apply sales conversion system. Just five stages, and a choice of 10 sales conversion strategies, transform your conversion of referrals and in particular general marketing enquiries.

Over a short period of time you should be averaging well over 70% for general marketing enquiries and 85% plus for referral enquiries.

Maximising Fees From Clients

- The 12% increase was achieved by reducing client losses, adding value and selling more value-added services.

Our Comments:

The Accountants Growth Programme comes with ready-to-go and easy-to-apply strategies for maximising fee income from clients. These little-known tactics work wonders when you apply them correctly.

PUTTING IT ALL TOGETHER

THE 'HARD' WAY OR THE 'EASY' WAY – IT'S YOUR CHOICE

SUMMARY

We've now taken you through the steps you need to take to quickly grow your accountancy firm. What you will have realised as you read each section was that, unfortunately, it takes time and effort to get good and consistent results.

We appreciate time, knowledge and expertise in marketing are resources which most accountants are not blessed with, but if you dedicate the time to implementing, learning, testing and generally becoming an expert in sales and marketing you can achieve results.

The question we leave you with is this...

Do you have the time to do it yourself?

If the answer is 'Yes' and you want to go through the process of trial and error, we genuinely wish you great success. You'll deserve it.

However, if you're like most of the partners we meet, you're so busy working in the business that the growth of your firm, although important to you, often takes a back seat. Sure, things get done intermittently but you're constantly fighting to keep things on track. It's just not that easy.

But there is a better, proven and easier way. You can take the short cut to success. You can join the Accountants Growth Programme and immediately start to see results.

Your first step is simple, risk-free and of course without obligation. Simply visit...

www.academyforgrowth.co.uk/pages/agp-video/

...and watch a special video presentation we've prepared, which gives you all the details about the programme.

Look... if you're NOT happy with the growth of your firm or it's not growing as fast as you want—THIS IS FOR YOU.

We give you our absolute assurance, you won't have seen anything like this before (guaranteed).

But you need to be quick. We have limited the number of memberships and they are filling up fast.

The video presentation lasts just over 30 minutes. No matter how busy you are right now, we promise the time you take to watch the video will be time very well spent.

Watch the video now...

www.academyforgrowth.co.uk/pages/agp-video/

Thanks again for investing in this book and we wish you every success growing your firm.

Getting In Touch

Steve & Richard Can Be Contacted In Several Ways

Contacting The Authors:

Steve and Richard would be delighted to hear from you especially with your success stories after reading and applying the steps in this book.

They can be reached by...

Telephone: 0844 44 80 640 (UK)
+44 1625 88 65 88 (International)

E-mail: steve.hackney@academyforgrowth.co.uk

richard.brewin@academyforgrowth.co.uk

Notes

Notes

Notes

Notes

Notes

NOTES

NOTES

NOTES

NOTES.

Notes

Notes

NOTES

Notes

Notes

Notes

Notes

Notes